WHAT'S A NICE REPUBLICAN GIRL LIKE ME DOING IN THE ACLU?

★★

WHAT'S A NICE REPUBLICAN GIRL LIKE ME DOING IN THE ACLU?

★★★

SHEILA SUESS KENNEDY

 Prometheus Books

59 John Glenn Drive
Amherst, NewYork 14228-2197

Published 1997 by Prometheus Books

01 00 99 98 97   5 4 3 2 1

Library of Congress Cataloging-in-Publication Data

Kennedy, Sheila Suess.
    What's a nice Republican girl like me doing in the ACLU? / Sheila
Suess Kennedy.
        p.   cm.
    ISBN 1–57392–143–2 (alk. paper)
    1. Civil rights—United States. 2. American Civil Liberties Union.
3. Indiana Civil Liberties Union. 4. Republican Party (U.S. : 1854–   )
I. Title.
JC599.U5K44   1997
323'.0973—dc21   97–7935
                                                          CIP

Printed in the United States of America on acid-free paper

Dedication

This book is dedicated to all of the people who sustain my faith in the human capacity for goodness, but especially to:

My children, stepchildren, and grandchildren, for whose sake I keep working, however inadequately, for a better world;

My husband, Bob, whose love, patience, and generosity of spirit are a constant gift;

My best friend, Jan, who has spent the last thirty years providing me with intellectual companionship and emotional support;

My mentor and friend P. E. MacAllister, who is the best example of citizenship I know;

And of course, to Barry Goldwater, who defined the term "Republican" for my generation.

Contents

★★

8   SHEILA SUESS KENNEDY

1

What's Wrong with This Picture?

★★

In 1980, I was a conservative Republican candidate for the U.S. Congress. In 1992, I accepted my current position as Executive Director of the ICLU—the Indiana affiliate of the American Civil Liberties Union. I was a three-day wonder.

A local alternative paper ran a huge red headline that proclaimed, "ICLU Taken Over by Card Carrying Republican!" Shortly thereafter, I received a letter of resignation from an ICLU member who cited my politics as sufficient reason to question the commitment and possibly the sanity of the board that hired me— after all, no one who had supported George Bush could possibly be a civil libertarian, a defender of the liberties enshrined in the Bill of Rights. A good friend on the staff of U.S. Senator Richard Lugar (R-Ind.) told me, in all seriousness, that when people asked him what in the world had come over me, he defended me by saying, "Sheila has paid her dues to the Republican party and she can do whatever she wants." Including, presumably, losing my mind.

It is undoubtedly a measure of my naivete that all this astonished me.

I have been, as they say, a "card carrying member" of the ACLU since 1967, and a politically active Republican since 1964. During all that time, I have considered the two affiliations entirely consistent.

I call myself a Goldwater Republican, which I define as generally libertarian: a philosophy characterized by the belief that government power is easily misused, and thus must be carefully monitored and limited. This is not libertarianism-*cum*-anarchy; government is clearly a necessary mechanism through which a citizenry establishes order and provides for the common welfare. Rather, it is a recognition that concentrated power, even in the hands of the most benign and well-meaning of functionaries (perhaps *especially* in such hands), is a potential threat to individual freedom. If liberty is something we value, prudence requires that we limit the ability of the state to interfere with a citizen's personal or economic choices. Overall, despite occasional lapses, this has been the message of the GOP.

The same logic impelled my membership in the ACLU. If one believes in markets for goods, surely markets for ideas are equally desirable. Liberty is not a divisible commodity. How secure is my property from a government that can forbid me to associate with certain people, or read certain books? How secure are any of my rights, political or economic, against a government that can decide who shall enjoy liberty and who shall not? The issue is the same—the power of the state.

It is absolutely true that some liberal Democrats are civil libertarians. This has always puzzled me, since they seem perfectly willing to limit individual rights in the service of their economic goals. It is equally true that in some parts of the country, theocrats have taken control of the Republican party apparatus. As a general rule, however, Democrats have been more willing to hand power to government than have Republicans, and by that logic, most members of the ACLU should be Republicans. But logic, I have discovered, is irrelevant.

I have spent the past three and a half years explaining the Civil Liberties Union to Republican friends who were astonished to find that a good portion of the ICLU Board of Directors is Republican. In the process, I have found that very few people know what civil liberties are. Fewer have ever read the Bill of Rights—let alone the Federalist and Antifederalist arguments that accompanied its adoption. Fewer still are familiar with the constitutional jurisprudence that ensued.

In the late 1960s, a number of universities around the country conducted experiments to gauge public knowledge of our constitutional system. In Indianapolis, political science students took clipboards to Monument Circle, the center of downtown Indianapolis. On each clipboard was a document titled "Petition to the Government." Beneath that heading was the text of the first ten amendments to the Constitution of the United States—the Bill of Rights. People were asked if they would sign the petition. I am told that 64 percent of those who were stopped refused to sign on the grounds that the petition was communist propaganda, or similarly subversive.

I had read about these experiments and, shortly after assuming my position at the ICLU (in 1992), I decided to replicate them. Resources and volunteers were scarce, and we ended up sending a lone volunteer to a local mall with the infamous clipboard. We titled our document "Petition" and faithfully reproduced the Bill of Rights. (Admittedly, we didn't print it on parchment, and we didn't write "Congress" using big s's, but otherwise it was exactly the same.) Our volunteer was instructed to record only *recognition*—not agreement. Of the thirty-three people who actually stopped and read the Bill of Rights, *only one recognized it.* (The good news is, it was a police officer.) I began to understand the magnitude of my problem: People who believe that the Bill of Rights is subversive are likely to believe that those of us defending it are equally subversive.

Three major misconceptions account for a great deal of hostility to the ACLU. The first is what I call "endorsement confusion." For some reason, people really have difficulty separating the defense of someone's rights from an endorsement of the way he or she exercises those rights. The ACLU can defend your right to read books of your own choosing without approving of the books you choose. We can oppose both the government's attempt to control pop music lyrics and the content of the lyrics. The issue is not what decision is made; the issue is *who decides?* In a free country, people will make decisions of which I do not approve. Some of those decisions will be harmful or annoying. But the alternative is to allow government to make them—a far more dangerous proposition.

This brings us to misconception number two, the notion that the Bill of Rights was intended to protect us against all unjust treatment. Private parties cannot violate one's civil liberties. Only government can. The Bill of Rights is a limitation on *government* action. The liberties secured to each of us are secured against *government* infringement. As I tell my Republican friends, the ICLU only sues the government, because only the government can violate your civil liberties. We are *not* shielded from all unjust treatment by the Bill of Rights.

For example, civil rights laws were passed because the Fourteenth Amendment did not protect racial minorities from private acts of discrimination, but only from invidious acts by government.

The third and most troubling misunderstanding is also the most fundamental: People believe that the United States is a majoritarian democracy. I frequently speak to high school classes, and I usually begin by saying, "This is America, so the majority rules, right?" Virtually every time, all the hands shoot up and heads nod. "So," I continue, "You can vote to make me Episcopalian, right?" This generates some confusion. They know they cannot take a vote to compel me to join a particular church, but they really don't know why. The reason, of course, is that we do not have pure democracy in America—we have representative democracy, with a libertarian "brake." That brake is the Bill of Rights, and it limits what government can do *even if the majority authorizes it.* So we cannot take a vote to decide what prayer you will say, what book you will read, what groups you will associate with. A city cannot decide, by popular vote, to abolish trial by jury, even if 99 percent of the voters believe the courts are too expensive. The entire purpose of the Bill of Rights was to remove certain matters from the reach of popular opinion—what the nation's founders called the tyranny of the majority. Of course, the majority generally does not try to deny rights to attractive and popular people, so the ACLU ends up representing some fairly unpleasant folks.

While I have been disappointed to find that a number of Republicans hold wildly inaccurate opinions about the ACLU, I have been equally frustrated by the prejudices of many ACLU members against Republicans.

Barely four months after I became executive director of the Indiana affiliate, I attended my very first meeting of the Executive Directors Council—a biennial gathering of affiliate directors from all over the country. It was my introduction to the organizational culture, and I will admit to an initial case of culture shock. I had packed what I believed to be appropriate attire for such a convention (what a national staff member later teased were my "little-old-lady-Republican knit suits"). I walked in to my first meeting—business suit, heels, control top pantyhose, and briefcase—only to encounter T-shirts, birkenstocks, beards, and backpacks. During business meetings, it became apparent that word of my political affiliation had gotten around; I was the object of very polite but unmistakable curiosity. Fortunately for me, Judith Mellon, the director of the Delaware affiliate, took me under her wing, introducing me around and generally acting as an interpreter. I found out later that several directors, upon meeting me, had predicted to her that I would never last.

In the years that have followed that first, somewhat unnerving, meeting, I have come to appreciate my colleagues on the staff of the ACLU. Rarely have I encountered a group of people who are more intelligent, informed, and genuinely caring. They are also scrupulously fair. These are qualities I do not take lightly. People work for the ACLU because they are passionate about individual freedom, and because the issues are more important than the notoriously low pay levels. If there are times when I feel like an ambassador to a foreign country, it is because so few of them have come to their positions from the business world. And just as the businesspeople with whom I worked had stereotypical notions about academics and public interest lawyers, the academics and public interest lawyers from whose ranks the ACLU staff is disproportionately drawn hold stereotypes about businesspeople and Republicans. If "intellectuals" are seen as impractical, "corporate types" are seen as self-serving and bigoted. There is just enough truth in each of these characterizations to make them difficult to root out. Even after four years, when I meet staff members for the first time, there will be a comment or offhand remark indicating that I am known as the Republican from Indiana—in the same way one might note the existence of a two-headed mule. Not that there is anything *wrong* with a two-headed mule, you understand. It's just unusual.

I have learned that these attitudes are neither political nor ideological. Very few of the staff members I know were ever politically active Democrats; virtually all of them celebrate the nonpartisan nature of the organization. Most agree with the director from a western state who begins his speeches with the assertion that the ACLU is the most conservative of organizations, because our mission is to *conserve* the values of the Constitution and the Bill of Rights. None of them has had any problem, to my knowledge, when we make a common cause of the drug war with the Cato Institute, a libertarian think tank, or even with the National Rifle Association, as we did on issues stemming from the 1993 tragedy in Waco.* These attitudes are a visceral response to cultural typecasting. Even though they know intellectually that all businesspeople are not Gordon Gekko and all Republicans are not Pat Bu-

---

*In April 1993, after a fifty-one-day siege, federal agents from the Bureau of Alcohol, Tobacco and Firearms stormed the compound of the Branch Davidians, a religious cult founded by David Koresh. The Davidians had been illegally stockpiling weapons and ammunition inside their Waco, Texas, stronghold. More than eighty cult members died in the attack, including Koresh himself and seventeen children.

chanan,* their personal experiences have not involved them with a more representative cross-section.

What is particularly ironic about both sets of misconceptions—those held by Republicans about civil libertarians and those held by civil libertarians about Republicans—is that they obscure the fact that traditional Republicans and core civil libertarians really agree on most issues.

For example, both believe in limiting the power that the state may exercise over the individual. Both support the concept that majority rule must be subject to the restraints of the law; that certain rights are fundamental and should not be subject to the whim of voters, or to popular passions. Both believe that rights are individual; that is, that government has the obligation to treat each of us as individuals, and not as members of groups.

The political spectrum is not a straight line, with "liberals" on the far left and "conservatives" on the far right. Rather, it is a circle, where the far left and the far right touch. And the only thing the extremists on both sides are arguing over is whose agenda government should impose on the rest of us. There are certainly totalitarian elements on the Republican right, just as there are on the Democratic left. But in the libertarian middle, traditional Republicans and civil libertarians have a large—and largely unrecognized—common agenda. Those of us in the GOP who have recognized that commonality for years need to speak up, or we risk losing our political party to the autocrats and our legal system to the Democrats.

---

*Gordon Gekko was the contemptible capitalist played by Michael Douglas in the Oliver Stone film *Wall Street*. Pat Buchanan is the poster boy for the cultural conservatives and anti-free-traders on the fringes of the Republican party.

2

The Past as Prologue

★★★

My father was a Democrat and my mother was a Republican. While they respected each other's opinions, they were unwilling to "cancel" each other's vote, so elections were preceded by family discussions of the issues and candidates; those discussions usually led to a joint decision favoring the Republicans. (Honesty impels me to disclose that my mother has since defected. Appalled by the influence of the radical right, and equally unable to embrace the economics of the Democrats, she now describes herself as a disenfranchised independent.) While both my parents cared about issues, they were not politically active. Neither was involved in political party organization; if they ever attended a City Council meeting or similar governmental function, I am not aware of it. They were just good citizens.

My father was a small businessman, and he was suspicious of "politicians" as a class. For a long time he was genuinely disturbed by the depth of my political involvement. He failed to realize that my political activism grew out of the values he had taught me and my sister: If you believe in something, you do something about it. You "put your money where your mouth is." He was unfailingly critical of people who were "all talk and no walk." In our small town, people came to him with their problems, knowing he would help with practical solutions (usually cash).

My mother did not work outside the home. She kept house and raised my younger sister and me. She was determined that we would be college-educated and independent; mother was a strong believer in women's rights. During the thirty-some years she lived in the small town of Anderson, Indiana, where ours was one of only thirty Jewish families, she served as president of numerous volunteer organizations. She was the one chosen to represent the Jewish families when the local elementary school celebrated Easter with a religious program explaining, among other things, that the Jews had killed the Lord. (The only other Jewish child in my school, a shy, blond girl named Beverly, refused to return to school for several days afterward.) My mother believed in her constitutional rights—and she also believed that asserting them was her civic responsibility, that you couldn't expect people to understand your position if you didn't explain it to them.

In college, I participated in the usual political discussions, but my first involvement with a real campaign came with the presidential candidacy of Barry Goldwater. I read *The Conscience of a Conservative*,[1] I listened to his speeches, and I signed on—stuffing envelopes and licking stamps at a local GOP headquarters. It was my first experience with a political organization, as opposed to political philosophy, and I was hooked. It was exciting being with others who shared my opinions, and it was good to feel that we were actually doing something to further our cause. I can still remember how angry I was when the infamous television commercial for Lyndon Johnson first aired—the one showing the little girl picking a daisy being blown to bits by an atomic bomb. (As a friend wryly remarked after the election, "They told me if I voted for Goldwater, we'd be in Vietnam. They were right. I did, and we are.") It was the first of many experiences I can only characterize as cognitive dissonance: a wide gap between the reality I experienced and the description of that reality by others. Years later, as a government official, I would get much the same feeling reading news accounts of public meetings I had attended and wondering whether the reporter and I had been at the same event.

The Goldwater positions that attracted me stressed personal autonomy and the obligation of government to respect individual freedom. I was also struck by the fact that Goldwater grounded discussion of his positions in a context that was missing from other campaigns—consideration of the proper role of government. The question to be asked was not "Is this a good idea?" Rather, the question was "Is this something *government* should do?" Beginning with the threshold question "What is the proper role of the state?" seemed absolutely reasonable to me then, and it still seems reasonable to me today.

Participation in the Goldwater campaign, even at so lowly a level, had made me feel that I was contributing to the process. The following year, by now a young housewife pregnant with my second child, I agreed to chair my township's Republican neighborhood finance campaign. Child number three arrived in time for the first of Richard Lugar's two campaigns for mayor of Indianapolis; I headed a group called "The 71 Committee for

Lugar for Mayor" (so named because it was 1971 and it would have been awkward to call ourselves "Jewish voters for Lugar," which is what we were). Most of the people I met in the course of these grassroots political activities were very much like me: We were housewives, laborers, small businesspeople, lawyers, and teachers all working for candidates we felt had demonstrated a commitment to good government. We shared a broad philosophical agreement, but in those days we imposed no litmus tests. It was accepted that reasonable people who believed generally in limited government and market economics might disagree on specific programs or issues without forfeiting the right to call themselves Republican.

On the other hand, while it is tempting to characterize the radical right's current insistence upon ideological purity as a phenomenon new to the GOP, that really wouldn't be accurate. Although their numbers and influence have grown, there has always been a tension in the party between those who embrace a libertarian ideology and those authoritarians who identify as Republicans because they see the Democrats as the party of "special interests," meaning blacks, Jews, labor unions, and other so-called liberal claimants to a piece of the political pie. I first encountered that intraparty tension in a state senate race in 1972.

Redistricting had resulted in a single senate district that included three incumbents. George Rubin was a lawyer and political moderate who had been responsible for the passage in Indiana of the Uniform Consumer Credit Code.* He supported the Equal Rights Amendment and reproductive rights. He was also the incum-

---

*This is a model set of laws eventually adopted in all states, setting out the rights of merchants and consumers, and regularizing enforcement of those rights and obligations.

bent slated by the local Republican organization; that is, he was the choice of the precinct committee members and party leadership. Traditionally, nonslated candidates had accepted the judgment of the slating committee and had withdrawn, avoiding contested primaries. One of the other incumbents did so; the third, Joan Gubbins, refused, and ran against the slate.

Gubbins was a self-described "good conservative Christian." She opposed the Equal Rights Amendment, reproductive freedom, and sex education, and she employed many of the tactics we have come to expect from latter-day extremists, but which were a new experience for most of us on the Rubin campaign. She characterized George as a "liberal Jew" and made constant references to her own brand of conservative Christianity. When the local chapter of the Women's Political Caucus endorsed George (the first and to my knowledge the only time the local organization actually endorsed a male over a female candidate), she pointed to the endorsement as proof that he was in league with "radical feminists." She won. It was a campaign that would have made Pat Robertson* and Pat Buchanan proud.

During the Rubin campaign, although I was a full-time law student with three small sons, I also worked on the campaign of William H. Hudnut III, a local Presbyterian minister who was the Republican party's choice for Indiana's eleventh congressional district seat. He was also opposed in the primary, and won nomination by a mere eighty-two votes. He went on to serve one term in the U.S. House of Representatives and four terms as mayor of Indianapolis. I worked on

---

*Pat Robertson founded the Christian Coalition, a political religious movement associated with the far right of the Republican party.

each of his campaigns, and in 1977, three years after my graduation from law school, Hudnut appointed me corporation counsel, or chief lawyer for the City of Indianapolis. For the first time, I was part of government rather than a political organization. As the first woman to hold the position, I was painfully aware of the need to prove myself.

If I had harbored any doubts about the importance of civil liberties and limited government, my experiences at City Hall would have resolved them. The announcement of my appointment came in the middle of a controversy over the annual display of a crèche on Monument Circle. Monument Circle is owned and maintained by the State of Indiana. The crèche in question was owned by the city and erected annually by the parks department. When the Indiana Civil Liberties Union and the Indianapolis Jewish Community Relations Council wrote to the mayor raising the issue of separation of church and state, a political firestorm erupted. Local letters to the editor were printed that were viciously anti-Semitic; community organizations called upon the mayor to protect "tradition"—although they took care not to specify whose. Hudnut could have made enormous political capital out of an impassioned defense of the display; to his credit, he refused to play politics with the issue. Told that the Constitution prohibits the use of tax dollars to endorse religious beliefs or promote religious observances, he ordered the display sold to a private organization. When I took over my new position at city legal, a deputy corporation counsel informed me that the sale would close as soon as he was able to "determine the fair market value of a plastic baby Jesus."

The crèche eventually was moved to the lawn of Christ Church Cathedral, still on the Circle but across from the

Monument. As recently as Christmas 1995, a caller to a local radio show complained that it "wasn't the same."

My stint at city legal also coincided with the emergence of the "Moral Majority," Jerry Falwell's attempt to mobilize conservative Christians. An Indianapolis minister, the Rev. Greg Dixon, served as national treasurer of the organization. Dixon headed a large congregation on the south side of town, and his members were particularly influential in south side city council districts. I had not been corporation counsel for very long when he prevailed upon a city council representative to introduce an ordinance to ban all rock concerts in city parks.

When new ordinances are proposed, the city legal staff is supposed to review them for form and legality. I dutifully attended the committee hearing at which the proposal to ban concerts was to be heard; in addition to the parks committee members, five or six members of the public were in attendance. One of them—a middle-aged woman in white anklets who periodically waved a small American flag—I later learned was a well-known neighborhood activist. The ordinance was called up for discussion, and I informed the committee that it could not constitutionally be enforced, since it was clearly an attempt by government to ban a particular type of message—what we lawyers refer to as "content-based" discrimination. I answered three or four questions from the committee and had turned to leave, when I was confronted by a stocky, dark-haired man who was literally trembling with rage. "You just stay where you are!" he commanded. "I am a taxpayer and you work for me, and I am here to tell you that my Bible is more important than your Constitution." The activist in the anklets waved her flag approvingly, and the other onlookers applauded.

The man who confronted me was later identified as

Greg Dixon. I cannot recall my response, although it must have been sufficient to convince the council committee, since the ordinance did not pass. (A measure addressing legitimate concerns about sanitation and crowd control at concerts did eventually go through, with legal division approval.) But I have never forgotten the encounter. His attack was an early example of what has become an increasingly common approach to the role of government. It was the expression of someone who knew—absolutely and unquestionably—what was good for me and for everyone else. If there are those who fail to act in accordance with the truth that has been revealed to him, then government must step in to insure our "correct" behavior. If "his" Bible tells him that rock music is evil, government must protect us from its influence. And if "my" Constitution gets in the way—well, it will just have to go.

A good friend once told me that everyone should work for government for at least two years—and be prohibited from doing so for longer than four years. Two years is long enough to learn to appreciate the complexities of the democratic process and to recognize the dangers of easy answers. After four years, you become part of the problem. While I am not entirely persuaded by the "term limits" part of his advice, I agree absolutely that government service provides insights that are difficult to acquire otherwise.

During my three-year tenure at city legal, we negotiated consent decrees growing out of allegations of race and sex discrimination in the police and fire departments. We dealt with constant changes in the CETA program (the Comprehensive Education and

Training Act), an early job training program for the poor and unskilled. It was my first experience with the federal government's tendency to fund the latest "fad" without giving much thought to the ability of local governments to apply the funds effectively, or the effect of the program on the private sector. I saw firsthand the problems created by overzealous or overworked bureaucrats pursuing even the worthiest of goals—I have vivid memories of environmental regulators whose "mathematical models" told them that we had carbon dioxide emissions that on-site measuring devices could not detect. And I also saw how political ambition influenced decisions of trial lawyers on my staff. Targeting "sin" was a sure crowd-pleaser; closing down a "dirty" bookstore was guaranteed to get headlines, while reporters ignored contracts for major redevelopment projects and other decisions having a far greater impact on our citizens. My years as corporation counsel provided me with a first-class, real-world look at government in action, and I am still grateful for the education.

I left city legal early in 1980 to run for the United States Congress. It was my first and last attempt at elective office. My opponent was Andrew Jacobs Jr., at the time a sixteen-year incumbent and a formidably popular Democrat. Of the five Republican primary candidates, I was the only woman, and women candidates—particularly women with young children—were still something of a novelty. Except for my gender, however, I was a pretty typical Republican candidate. The following is taken verbatim from the introduction to my position papers:

> There is no area where the difference between Republicans and Democrats is more pronounced than with respect to the approach of each to social issues. The

Democrats' position has consistently been to throw public money at social problems. More and bigger federal programs, federal regulations, and federal mandates have characterized the Democrats' approach.

The following papers are consistent with a Republican philosophy, which differs markedly in its emphasis. Far from being unconcerned or indifferent to the problems of the disadvantaged, Republicans have understood that the welfare of those who are marginal in our society depends in large part on the economic and social health of the society as a whole. We have recognized the need to fashion programs which will bring the disadvantaged into the mainstream, rather than encouraging continued dependency. We see a need for greater consistency, so that, for example, programs designed to strengthen families are not undermined by tax policies which have the opposite effect. And finally, we are concerned with the effect of too much government intrusion into the private and everyday affairs of our citizens.

The position papers that followed dealt primarily with economic issues—unemployment, equal opportunity, welfare, and the like. By far the greatest emphasis was on national defense, as we were still fighting the cold war. Issues we think of as "social issues" today were virtually absent from the campaign; although I was prochoice and supported equal rights for gays and lesbians, relatively little attention was paid to those positions.

I won the primary fairly easily, but lost the general election to Jacobs. While it may seem ironic in today's political context, I was viewed by many voters as far too conservative. My emphasis on national defense probably had something to do with that image. The campaign ran three rather grim television ads showing me with—respectively—a B-52 bomber, a tank, and several surface-to-air missiles, warning of the need to maintain an adequate defense posture. (While I lost the election, I have always credited those ads with bringing in divorce clients who wanted one really *mean* lawyer.)

Although I continued my involvement in party politics after my defeat, most of my energy was directed toward building my legal practice and raising my family. I concentrated on business and real estate law, so I was initially surprised when in 1983 I was contacted by a New York law firm to act as local counsel for the American Booksellers Association in connection with a First Amendment issue.*

The Indianapolis City-County Council was considering an ordinance drafted by law professor Catherine MacKinnon and feminist author Andrea Dworkin. A very similar law had been passed by the Minneapolis City Council but vetoed by their mayor; in Indianapolis, Mayor Hudnut supported the measure and promised to sign it. The ordinance declared that "pornography" was sex discrimination subject to sanctions by the local Human Relations Commission and to civil actions by private parties. The American Booksellers Association, the Association of College Bookstores, and a variety of other parties opposed to passage were hoping to avoid the expense of a lawsuit by persuading the City Council to reject the ordinance, which was clearly unconstitutional. The opposition of a conservative female Republican with feminist credentials could only help.

When I first read the proposed ordinance, my reaction was bafflement. I could understand the enthu-

---

*Local counsel are lawyers who practice in a jurisdiction and are hired to assist the "foreign" lawyers primarily responsible for a representation.

siasm of some fundamentalist churches for the measure; they were intent upon ridding the city of sexually explicit books and movies. Not being lawyers, they might not have recognized its constitutional infirmities. But I couldn't understand how such a proposal could have been produced by liberal feminists; to my eyes, the measure was profoundly antiwoman.

The basic thrust of the ordinance was to define as "pornographic" any sexually explicit representation that "degraded" or "subordinated" women. None of these terms was defined with any precision; indeed, they seemed almost deliberately subjective and overly broad. Even a determination that a picture was sexually explicit could rest on "a context which makes such representations sexual." Both William Shakespeare's *Taming of the Shrew* and Janemarie Luecke's *The Rape of the Sabine Women* would have been encompassed by the language. Anyone claiming to have been harmed by the publication of "pornographic" material (assuming one could figure out what it was) could bring a civil suit against the author, producer, distributor, or seller. Since the First Amendment protects the transmittal of ideas (including bad ideas), the ordinance simply pronounced that these particular ideas were *acts* rather than *speech*. I couldn't help thinking of Alice talking to Humpty-Dumpty after she traveled "through the looking glass": When *I* use a word, it means what *I* want it to mean!

It was my first encounter with the "gender feminism" that Christina Hoff Sommers described so accurately several years later in her book *Who Stole Feminism?*[2] ("Gender feminism" abandons the early feminists' insistence on equal treatment in favor of special rights for women.) At the time I understood only that there were women who did not see themselves as free and equal participants in the intellectual or economic marketplaces, and who obviously did not seek such equality as their goal. The ordinance itself, and the arguments in support of it, characterized women as childlike and helpless. Men were described as barely restrained sexual predators, whose least encounter with "pornography" would unleash their true nature and impel them to rape and mutilate. Only if government intervened to banish the bad ideas could we poor, weak, little women be saved.

The council sponsor of the measure was Beulah Coughenour, a Republican who had opposed passage of the Equal Rights Amendment, and who had never publicly expressed an interest in women's rights. She had spoken out frequently against "pornography," however, and was a reliable vote for government restrictions on free speech. Although she parroted much of the MacKinnon/Dworkin leftist rhetoric about protecting women, the ordinance garnered no support from local women's rights organizations.

Members of the City Council had moved to limit debate on the ordinance, and allowed only three people to testify: Sam Jones, Executive Director of the Urban League; William Marsh, a constitutional law professor and vice-president of the Indiana Civil Liberties Union; and me. I was extended this courtesy only because I had recently been a member of the city administration. Each of us urged rejection of the ordinance, to the clear displeasure of those in the crowded public assembly hall. Busloads of antismut crusaders had been brought in by local churches, and their influence over the uncomfortable officials was unmistakable. As one councilman said rather regretfully in a brief speech explaining his vote, "I have a lot of respect for Mrs. Kennedy's opinion that the ordinance is unconstitutional, but I'm against pornography."

Perhaps the most telling aspect of the council meeting occurred after the ordinance had passed. Rozelle Boyd, a Democrat and Indiana University Dean who had voted against passage, moved to limit the amount the city could spend defending the ordinance to $200,000. His motion was voted down, and the city ended up paying a great deal more than that before the case concluded. But Rozelle had made his point; the majority was willing to squander tax dollars defending something that most of them knew to be indefensible, because it was politically expedient.

The American Booksellers Association immediately brought suit, and Judge Sarah Evans Barker of the U.S. District Court for Southern Indiana ruled the ordinance unconstitutional. In language that laid bare the fatal flaw in the logic of the proponents, she wrote,

> If this court were to accept defendants' argument—that the State's interest in protecting women from the humiliation and degradation which comes from being depicted in a sexually subordinate context is so compelling as to warrant the regulation of otherwise free speech to accomplish that end—one wonders what would prevent the City-County Council (or any other legislative body) from enacting protections for other equally compelling claims against exploitation and discrimination. . . . Legislative bodies . . . could also enact legislation prohibiting other unfair expression —the publication and distribution of racist material, for instance, on the grounds that it causes racial discrimination, or legislation prohibiting ethnic or religious slurs on the grounds that they cause discrimination against particular ethnic or religious groups. . . . It ought to be remembered by defendants and all others who would support such a legislative initiative that, in terms of altering sociological patterns, much

as alteration may be necessary or desirable, free speech, rather than being the enemy, is a long-tested and worthy ally.

The decision was upheld at the Seventh Circuit, and the city appealed to the United States Supreme Court. Such appeals, called "appeals for *certiorari*"* are rarely granted. Typically, the Supreme Court will do one of two things: refuse to hear a case and allow the lower court's ruling to stand (where it will be a controlling precedent only within that appellate court's jurisdiction); or the Court will accept a case for review and issue a full opinion. Instead, the Supreme Court issued a simple, unanimous, one-line order affirming the Seventh Circuit opinion. The summary disposition was an eloquent affirmation of free speech and a clear message that similar measures should not be attempted in other parts of the country. It was a stunning rebuke to the ordinance's proponents.

There were obviously many lessons to be learned from *American Booksellers* v. *Hudnut,* but perhaps the most important was that censors come from all parts of the political spectrum. Left-wingers want to impose politically correct attitudes and "sensibilities." Right-wingers want to protect us from sin. Both want to be the ones who decide which words, pictures, and ideas don't measure up.

My representation of the plaintiffs in *American Booksellers,* although I was only local counsel, had strained my relationship with Bill Hudnut. Despite a number of conversations, he never understood why the

---

Certiorari is an order issuing from a higher court, such as the U.S. Supreme Court, to a lower one and calling up the records and proceedings in some cause for review or a speedier judgment.

ordinance was so dangerous. But other threats to individual liberty were easier for him to see. His commitment to the fight against racial discrimination was genuine and deeply felt, and his belief in a woman's right to reproductive freedom was equally strong. That commitment to choice was tested during his last term as mayor, when he and his wife, Beverly, found that the eagerly anticipated first child of their marriage was so severely defective that it could not live more than a few hours after birth. Beverly was in her fifth month when they received the diagnosis; after much prayer and anguish, they terminated the pregnancy. Most people were understanding, although there were a few "letters to the editor" in the local paper condemning the "murder" of their "preborn son." Their experience added to their frustration with the GOP platform's antichoice provisions. It wasn't only that they considered the platform plank inconsistent with traditional Republican philosophy respecting individual moral autonomy; they also decried its highly divisive effect within the party. In 1992, in the months leading up to the Republican National Convention, they headed up a national effort by prochoice Republicans (including my old hero, Barry Goldwater) called "The Unity Platform." The goal was to keep the party platform silent on the issue, remanding it to the consciences of individuals rather than to the dictates of the party or the state.

My involvement with their effort coincided with prochoice activities of my own. In 1989, the Supreme Court decided *Webster* v. *Reproductive Health Services*, in which it upheld the constitutionality of significant new restrictions on abortion. Several politically active women had been gathered by Cynthia Mahern, an aide to Representative Andrew Jacobs and the wife of a prominent Democratic state senator. We were a meticulously bipartisan group, half Republican, half Democrat. All of us were concerned by the Supreme Court's retreat from the principles of *Roe* v. *Wade*, the 1973 decision which legalized abortion. If the Court was going to give increasing latitude to state legislatures to interfere with a woman's reproductive choices, we would have to concentrate our efforts on our legislature. We decided to form the Indiana Women's Network for Political Action—a single-issue, prochoice, political action committee (PAC).

We wanted to send two messages to our state legislators: that the choice issue crossed political party lines and that women of both political parties were prepared to fund their convictions. Accordingly, the PAC had Republican and Democrat co-chairs, and committee membership was evenly divided between the parties. Charter members contributed a thousand dollars each to "seed" the PAC and to insure that we had the ability to support prochoice candidates at a meaningful level. We raised $140,000 the first six weeks, to the surprise and consternation of many male legislators. I served as the PAC's first Republican co-chair; later, my stepdaughter Kelly was the organization's only staff. She and I signed on to help the Hudnuts promote the Unity Platform, she as volunteer coordinator, me as a volunteer.

The efforts to enlist prochoice Republicans from all over the country began in earnest just weeks after I had moved to the ICLU. One of the organizers of the Unity Platform worked with a group called the Republican Mainstream Organization. As the name implies, the organization was formed to represent the views of mainstream Republicans whose voices had been increasingly obscured by the more strident (and newsworthy) rhetoric of the party's right wing. My contact shared a small office with the Ripon Society, another, older organization of moderate Republicans. Based in Washington, D.C., he sent a constant stream of polling and other data, and offered advice based upon a considerable knowledge of Republicans across the country. One day he called me and was surprised when the telephone was answered "ICLU." After verifying that I was, indeed, the executive director of an ACLU affiliate, he asked me what I had thought when George Bush called Michael Dukakis a "card carrying member of the ACLU."

I admitted that the tactic had made me angry, but said I had attributed it to thoughtlessness and the pressure of the campaign. "Not at all," he responded. "I worked in the White House during the campaign, and it may make you feel better to know that Bush refused four times to use that line before he finally agreed."

Actually, it made me feel a lot worse. It was emblematic of the intellectual dishonesty that pervades discussions of the ACLU. It reminded me—as if I needed reminding—that getting people in my party to understand civil liberties and the ACLU was not going to be easy. Just how far some GOP activists had strayed from the party's traditional values (ironically, in the name of "traditional values") became even clearer at the 1992 national convention. Those controlling the agenda refused even to allow discussion of the Unity Platform; the program showcased a disgraceful, homophobic screed by Pat Buchanan; and Bill Hudnut —who had served for sixteen years as mayor of the largest city in the U.S. headed by a Republican—was told by a delegate that he and other prochoicers "didn't belong" in the Republican party.

It had been thirty-two years since I had first read *The Conscience of a Conservative.* I had spent a considerable portion of those years working for a Republican party that I believed stood for the principles of limited government and individual liberty. Like many other Republicans who were dismayed and disheartened by the 1992 convention, I had to ask myself whether my loyalties belonged primarily to the political party, or to the philosophy.

I wanted to promote the principles that had drawn me to the Republican party in the first place. As an organization person, I knew that I had an obligation to work within the Republican party for a return to mainstream Republican values. As a libertarian, I realized that it was time to channel my energies through the ACLU.

NOTES

1. Barry Goldwater, *The Conscience of a Conservative* (Shepherdsville, Ky.: Victor Publishing, 1960).
2. Christina H. Sommers, *Who Stole Feminism? How Women Have Betrayed Women* (New York: Simon & Schuster, 1994).

3

Hanging Out on the Intake Line

★★★

I was really excited when the call came telling me that
the Board of Directors of the ICLU was offering me the
executive director's job. I had grown bored with private
practice, and a disastrous venture as a real estate de-
veloper had shown me that probusiness sentiments are
not the equivalent of business acumen. My children
were all self-supporting (rather precariously, in a couple
of cases, but self-supporting nonetheless). I wanted to
do something meaningful, even if it meant less income.
When the local newspaper reported that the ICLU was
looking for a new executive director, I told my husband
that I wanted to apply. He blanched when I told him the
salary, but once he recovered, he was his usual supportive self. (Living with me all these years clearly qualifies him for a medal; being enthusiastic about living
with me probably qualifies him for sainthood.)

I had never worked for a nonprofit organization, except as a volunteer or board member, and my first weeks

on the job were disorienting. Amid the odds and ends of cast-off furniture, stained carpeting, missing ceiling tiles, haphazard files, and ancient office equipment, volunteers answered telephones while I tried to cope with arcane manuals from the national office and a budget deficit all our own. More than once I found myself wondering what in the world I had gotten myself into.

Gradually, we pulled the office together. I was fortunate that the ICLU legal director had been with the organization for seven years and was an absolutely first-rate lawyer. The only other staff was a volunteer lawyer who traded twenty hours a week for office space and two secretaries. Together, we were responsible for a statewide membership organization. The legal staff handled all the litigation; but *only* litigation. Initially, I was the only staff person working on everything else—office administration, legislative work, educational programming, and of course fundraising. The ACLU and ICLU are almost entirely dependent upon private donations and membership dues; the only exception is the award of legal fees in the minority of cases where such fees are recoverable. In Indiana, fewer than a third of our cases have any fee potential, even if we win. And we never charge our clients.

Prior to becoming executive director, I had only the haziest notion of how the ICLU got involved with specific cases. Even though I had spent a brief time on the Indianapolis screening committee—a group of volunteer lawyers who review and investigate requests for ICLU assistance—I had really not given much thought to how the cases came in the door. Had someone asked me to estimate the number of people who called or wrote the organization asking for help, I would have guessed three or four a week; it came as a considerable shock to discover that the office receives in excess of fifteen *thou-*

sand calls each year from people requesting representation. Those requests generally come by telephone, through what we call the "Intake Line." This is a special telephone line staffed (on good days) by volunteers who determine whether the call warrants further ICLU action or referral to a more appropriate agency.

More surprising to me than the number of calls we received was the volume of complaints having absolutely nothing to do with civil liberties. The number of people who have been abducted by Martians—or the FBI—is astounding, and nearly all of them have had electrodes implanted in their brains. (I was always at a loss to deal with these calls until we got a volunteer who had spent time in the mayor's office, which must get a lot of similar complaints. She cheerfully tells the callers that aluminum foil will interrupt the transmissions. They are uniformly grateful for the advice.) When the Indiana Division of Natural Resources decided to allow a "deer shoot" to thin the deer population in a state park, we received at least a dozen calls from people who were indignant that we were not protecting the civil liberties of the deer! We had an equally querulous complaint from a woman who wanted the ICLU to sue to "stop all the fornication" because "studies show that fornication is more enjoyable than job training and that is why all these young women are on welfare." (We weren't exactly sure *who* we were supposed to sue, but a summer intern volunteered to participate in the "study.")

Perhaps my favorite Intake call was from an agitated female who insisted that "the judge" had violated her civil liberties. The volunteer on the phone politely asked how. "He told me to stop drinking," the caller explained. My volunteer was puzzled. "How did this violate your civil liberties?" The caller insisted that she had never taken a drink of alcohol in her life. The volunteer, by this time curious, asked, "If you have never taken a drink, why do you suppose the judge told you that?" "Why," responded the caller, "I suppose it is because one of the personalities with whom I share this body is a real lush!" As the humorist Dave Barry might say, I am not making this up.

When people think of the ACLU, they generally think of lawsuits. This is understandable. As we are fond of noting, the Bill of Rights is not self-executing; it cannot enforce itself. The ACLU was established to defend constitutional principles by filing lawsuits. When legislative bodies or governmental administrations act in ways our Constitution prohibits—when they break the rules—it is the function of the courts to correct them. But as every first-year law student learns, American courts cannot act in the absence of a "case or controversy." There must be a genuine dispute, between real parties with real interests at stake, before the courts can exercise jurisdiction. A given government action can be blatantly unconstitutional, but if no one challenges it, it will stand. I still remember discussions among city council members over proposals of dubious legality; someone would question a suggested ordinance and someone else would respond with "Who is going to complain?" It is the role of the ACLU to help people complain.

It bears emphasizing that we *help* people complain; we are not the plaintiffs in the lawsuits we bring. We are lawyers who "specialize" in constitutionally protected liberties. We supplement the work of private attorneys, who must make a living and thus must charge for representation. And because our first concern is the principle involved, we are often the only lawyers willing to represent unpopular (even despicable) people. A friend of mine summed it up nicely when he referred to the Constitution as our "most important client."

For a long time, the ACLU was primarily a public interest law firm. Although officers and staff wrote essays and gave lectures, although direct mail fundraising and membership recruitment necessitated a certain amount of educational content, these activities were seen primarily as supportive of the central mission: suing government agencies for constitutional violations.

By the time I joined the staff, the Washington, D.C., office had been established for many years, and lobbying legislative bodies on behalf of civil liberties had also become an important part of the ACLU mission. More recently, the organization has realized how really critical civic education is to the health of the polity in general and civil liberties in particular. Courts do not operate in a vacuum; judges reflect prevailing political and social attitudes toward the laws they interpret. Furthermore, our legal system depends upon voluntary compliance and respect for the rule of law. When popular culture rejects court-imposed rules, when the bases for decisions are not understood and the law is ignored or mocked, the entire structure of our legal system is weakened. Without an educated and informed citizenry, courts cannot continue to protect our liberties.

As important as lobbying and education have become, however, the ACLU's most enduring legacy is unquestionably the role we have played in shaping constitutional jurisprudence over the past seventy-five years. Americans would literally live in a different country today had it not been for the ACLU's insistence that we adhere to the principles of limited government established by the nation's founders.

In 1933, when the government tried to ban importation of James Joyce's *Ulysses* as obscene, the ACLU won a ruling that the First Amendment prohibited such censorship. When a 1925 law was passed in Tennessee making it a crime to teach evolution in the public schools, it was Clarence Darrow, a member of the ACLU national committee, who headed the team of volunteer lawyers. In the 1930s, when West Virginia adopted a resolution allowing the expulsion of public school students who refused to salute the flag, the ACLU represented the children of Jehovah's Witnesses whose religious beliefs forbade them to salute. In 1932, when the Scottsboro boys—nine black Alabama youths charged with raping two white women—were denied the assistance of counsel during a trial in which they were sentenced to death, the ACLU won a ruling that established the right of defendants to representation by a lawyer. In these and numerous other well-known cases, the ACLU has represented individuals against arbitrary and overreaching government action.

For every famous case that has gone to the U.S. Supreme Court and changed or confirmed a legal principle, the ACLU and its affiliates are involved in hundreds of other efforts to prevent abuses of power. When I came to the ICLU, we were just concluding a case on behalf of a group of senior citizens from Vincennes, a small town in southern Indiana. For years, the elderly plaintiffs had congregated daily at Sunset Center, a facility that had been used as a senior citizen center since the 1930s. When election time rolled around, the center typically sported campaign posters and literature; however, in the late 1980s, despite some not-so-thinly veiled warnings from the Vincennes Housing Authority (which owned the building), the seniors decided to oppose the incumbent mayor, who was running for re-election. They were determined to protest the level of city services in the poorer sections of town, including the section where the center was located. They hung posters and campaigned for the incumbent's opponents in both the primary and general elections. When the mayor won, his appointed Housing Authority announced it would close the center.

Not surprisingly, none of the handful of lawyers practicing in Vincennes, Indiana, was anxious to represent a group of low-income seniors against a just-reelected mayor and his administration. I certainly don't blame them. Had there not been an organization like the ICLU, however, there would have been nowhere for those elderly people to go. I know of few people who would argue that government officials ought to be able to condition municipal services on political support—but a right without a remedy is meaningless. If rules cannot be enforced, they may be nice platitudes, but they are no longer rules. For every high-profile, controversial case we take, there are ten like Sunset Center—which, thanks to the ICLU, is still open.

If I have been surprised by the number of cases involving government officials who really knew that their actions were not constitutionally defensible, but who figured that no one would complain, I have been touched and impressed by the courage it takes to be a plaintiff in some of these lawsuits. For some of our clients, the willingness to stand up for their beliefs comes at a considerable price.

Allen and Becky Berger live in Rensselaer, Indiana. When Allen discovered that Gideon Bibles were being distributed in his son's fifth grade public school classroom, he thought a simple letter to the superintendent would be enough to stop the practice. After all, the First Amendment just does not allow tax-supported schools to invite representatives of any religious order to proselytize to young students who are a captive audience. But the school board ignored the advice of its own lawyer, voted to continue Bible distribution, and publicly rebuked the Bergers for having the effrontery to raise the issue. During the nearly three years it took to litigate *Berger* v. *Rensselaer*, Allen and Becky were the focus of a good deal of unwelcome attention in their small town. Even though Becky is an elder in the local Presbyterian church, they were accused of hostility to religion; they received hate mail; and some formerly friendly neighbors stopped speaking to them. The principle they vindicated was sufficiently important to both of them to make the unpleasantness worthwhile. As Allen said at a meeting not too long ago, "The religious formation of our children is for *us* to determine—not the state."*

In cases like *Berger* and *Sunset Center*, the principle at stake is obvious. Frequently, however, we will get involved in a case that seems at first glance to be trivial—even frivolous. A Republican friend with whom I often debate is given to dismissing these suits with "Oh, get a life!" or "Who cares? Why should the courts waste time on *that*?" Of course, he is a privileged, Harvard-educated, white lawyer for whom the system has always worked. But the question is a fair one, even if the manner of raising it leaves something to be desired. Why would an organization with limited resources choose to represent a fifth grade student suspended from public school for wearing an earring? Why would we "waste" resources defending the right of a tavern owner to offer topless dancing? In the broad scheme of things, are these really issues worth arguing about? Who cares? The answer

---

*For a detailed description of the ACLU involvement in this and similar school prayer cases, see Robert S. Alley, *Without a Prayer: Religious Expression in Public Schools* (Amherst, N.Y.: Prometheus Books, 1996).

is: We should all care. Not about earrings or topless dancers, but about the genuinely important principles involved in these seemingly trivial disputes.

As I write this, the ICLU is representing a young boy named Jimmy Hines against his rural school system. Jimmy idolizes his father, who for several years has worn an earring. When Jimmy was in the fifth grade, his mother gave him and his dad a set of diamond ear studs—one for each of them. Jimmy wore his for several months without incident, but then the school authorities decided that wearing the stud constituted "cross-dressing" and could no longer be tolerated. Jimmy was given an ultimatum—forego the earring or forego school.

No one at the ICLU questions the right of school systems to adopt and enforce rules ensuring the safety of students and teachers, or promoting an environment conducive to education. But rules must bear some rational relationship to the educational mission of the school. They should also be respectful of the rights and prerogatives of parents insofar as possible. When a public school—an arm of government—decides to override parental authority, we expect that school to have a good reason. The issue in the case of Jimmy Hines is not the propriety of a boy wearing an earring. The issue is who decides whether he wears an earring? Is this a proper exercise of the power of the state? Or does it invade the province of the family? If the latter, what does that say about government's respect for "family values"? (Is it possible we only expect government to defer to "family values" when the majority agrees with the values of the particular family involved?) Just how intrusive must government get before we draw the line?

Abuse of government power was also the issue in the case involving the topless dancers. The tavern owner operated a bar on the outskirts of a small town. He had installed strippers in an effort to improve business and it worked; the bar was doing well. He was in compliance with all of the applicable rules and regulations established by local ordinance and the Alcoholic Beverage Commission.

Members of the town board were approached by members of the local Christian Coalition, who disapproved of the bar's entertainment. At their urging, and despite legal advice that they would be violating the owner's rights, they passed an ordinance making topless dancing illegal. The ordinance was to take effect one month following passage; the idea that fairness might at least require time for the owner to amortize his considerable investment in the property evidently never crossed the minds of those who drafted the measure. The owner contacted the ICLU, we sued, the town settled, and the bar continues to operate.

The plaintiff is a small businessman. He was operating his business within the law; he was in full compliance with a whole array of fairly onerous regulations. His customers chose to patronize his establishment—residents who didn't approve of his entertainment were under no pressure to go. If—as the town board charged—the tavern's business was inconsistent with local community standards, surely business would have been less robust. In fact, it was precisely because a market existed for the tavern's topless shows that the town board acted. It used government's zoning power to destroy a business because some of the town's residents disapproved of what other residents were watching. Today, topless dancers. Tomorrow—what?

Cases like these create the same dilemma as the bully on the playground. Do you stand up to him when he first starts bossing you around, or do you wait until he really hurts you? Teachers who have pulled a lot of playground duty will tell you that the more powerful the bully, the more important it is to enforce rules promptly and consistently. The role of the ACLU is a lot like the role of the teacher on that playground. We are there to be sure that the big kid follows the rules.

4

The Great Prayer Wars

★★

May I offer a prayer for a little good will and intellectual honesty in the ongoing war over the meaning of the First Amendment religion clauses? I have discovered that both are in very short supply.

The First Amendment prohibits government from "establishing" religion. Courts and historians have agreed that "establishment" means to endorse, sponsor, or otherwise favor any particular religion *or* religion itself. Government is also prohibited from interfering with the "free exercise" of religion by individuals. That is, so long as a religious observance does not violate a law of general application meant to protect the rights of others, the government cannot prohibit it. Together, the Establishment Clause and Free Exercise Clause are a prescription for government neutrality in matters of conscience. It is not accidental that this language accompanies the free speech provisions of the First Amendment; in its entirety, that amendment guarantees our right to believe what we wish, associate with whomever we choose, say what we think, pray to the god of our choice or not—all free of government coercion.

In 1992, in *Lee* v. *Weisman,* the U.S. Supreme Court held that the Establishment Clause forbids government-sponsored prayer at public school graduations. Because it was an ACLU case, I held a press conference to announce the ruling and discuss its reasoning. One of the reporters asked me if I was surprised that conservative justices chosen by Republican presidents Reagan and Bush agreed with the ACLU on this issue. As I told him, a truly conservative court—a court determined to respect legal precedent and to *conserve* the principles of the Constitution and the Bill of Rights— could have done nothing else.

The Court had issued its ruling on June 24, too late to affect graduations in 1992. There were a few anguished editorials proclaiming the end of the world as we have known it, and one or two school officials publicly threatened defiance, but passions appeared to subside as the year wore on. It wasn't until the following March that all hell broke loose.

The American Center for Law and Justice, known as the ACLJ, is an unofficial arm of the Christian Coalition. Formed by Pat Robertson specifically to counter the "evil" ACLU, it is a legal organization intent upon reversing constitutional doctrines mandating government neutrality toward religion. In March 1993, the ACLJ sent a "legal memorandum" to every school district in the United States, urging school officials to continue prayer at graduation and "interpreting" *Lee* v. *Weisman* to allow such devotions so long as a clergyperson was not involved. The memorandum did not disclose the ACLJ's affiliation with the Christian Coalition, and in the opinion of most constitutional scholars, it significantly mischaracterized the holding in *Lee*. Telephones at the ICLU began ringing. Worried school officials felt caught between the proverbial rock and hard place. For months they had received warnings from their own lawyers and from various professional associations to avoid official prayer; now they had received a memorandum which implied that they could be subject to legal action if they removed prayer from the program. What was the ICLU position?

I conferred with Alex Tanford, a law professor who was then our vice-president for education. We decided that the ICLU should respond to these concerns with a letter of our own. Little did we know what our attempt at clarification would produce!

The ICLU letter began by referring to the ACLJ memorandum. We pointed out that it had been issued by an organization that was not disinterested, and should be read with that in mind. We detailed what we believed to be inaccuracies in the legal analysis, and we suggested a constitutionally acceptable alternative to the inclusion of prayer at the graduation ceremony—a separate, privately sponsored baccalaureate service. We emphasized the importance of school officials setting a good example for students by following the law, even a law they might not like. (After all, we expect high school students to obey laws with which they disagree.) And then we included the fateful warning: if schools willfully violated the law, they would probably be sued, and such suits can be very expensive to defend.

Neither Alex nor I had been active in the ICLU long enough to realize that, for a number of reasons (mostly having to do with institutional history) the organization was perceived by many as bellicose and litigious. Our statement that intentional constitutional violations

give rise to liability was seen not as a factual reminder,
but as a threat. Newspapers all over the state ran
headlines like "ICLU Warns: Pray and We'll Sue!" Obscene messages and death threats came in on the Intake line. ("God wants you dead," was a mild example.)
We received stacks of anonymous hate mail. One,
which began, "You Yids," concluded with, "the holo-
caust was too good for you." (As the only Jew on staff,
I took that one personally.) Pat Robertson held up our
letter on the "700 Club"—national television!—and pronounced me a tool of Satan. (This event has since become part of family folklore. My youngest son calls
himself "Satan's spawn." My architect husband
watched the show and in his very best I-told-you-so
manner, lectured me: "Now aren't you glad you listened
to me and had the ICLU letterhead redesigned? Think
how awful the old stationery would have looked on national television." They thought it was funny; I was be-
side myself with embarrassment and anger.) No one
seemed to remember that the ACLJ's memo had
started it all, and that we had merely responded.

As the graduation season unfolded, I began to understand that the media coverage did not reflect most
public opinion. I am still grateful for the call I got from
a school superintendent thanking the ICLU for clari-
fying the law, and for the support we received from a
number of school board lawyers who had felt pressured
by local citizens angry about the Supreme Court's decision. I was also gratified that very few Indiana communities defied the law. Instead, many took our advice
and opted for a separate baccalaureate service, sponsored not by government but by local churches.

I learned some very valuable lessons from what I
have come to call "the great prayer wars." Having discovered that the ICLU is regarded in some quarters as

the eight-hundred-pound gorilla, I am certainly more careful when I draft correspondence. More significantly, until the public outcry over graduation prayer, I had not realized how confused people are about the First Amendment and the doctrine of separation of church and state. I also had not understood that in some quarters, the confusion is deliberately cultivated. During the controversy over our letter, a local attorney who markets himself as a "Christian lawyer" faxed press releases to media around the state, offering free representation to any *student* sued by the ICLU for praying at graduation. To my knowledge, not a single newspaper or television reporter who ran the story made the obvious point that the offer was a sham, because individuals cannot violate the First Amendment. Only government can. We might have sued a school corporation, but we could not have sued a student. Such bare-faced tactics succeed only because the level of public understanding is so low.

On the theory that the best thing to do when handed a lemon is to make lemonade, Alex suggested we use the controversy as an opportunity for public education. He spent literally hundreds of hours on the telephone with school officials and lawyers from around the state; I gave interviews, participated in panel discussions, and wrote pieces for newspaper op-ed pages. "What Do We Teach the Children?" appeared in several Indiana newspapers and was intended to be my final word on the subject.

> People of good will can disagree, but if disputes are to be productive (that is, if they are to present us with opportunities to clarify positions and understand issues) there need to be ground rules. I suggest two:

1) Tell the truth. Argue about real differences—don't create "straw men" just because the issues you manufacture are easier to refute than the opinions the other guy actually holds.

2) Begin with the assumption that even people with whom you disagree may be (gasp!) good people. Don't demonize others just because they don't agree with you.

How would these rules apply to the current controversy over prayer at graduation? At a minimum, they would require us to define the real issues. What does the First Amendment say? What has the Supreme Court *said* the First Amendment says? If the Supreme Court is wrong, why? And what is appropriate action to take if one disagrees with the law?

In *Lee* v. *Weisman,* the Supreme Court said that public schools are a part of government and that government cannot make you pray. The Court also said that a majority cannot vote to overrule the Constitution. The reason the Bill of Rights was enacted was to protect individuals from the "tyranny of the majority." Your neighbors cannot vote to make you Episcopalian and high school students cannot vote to ignore the First Amendment.

The Court did *not* say that graduation speakers cannot refer to God, or that seniors cannot sing a song that mentions God. The Court did *not* say that a privately sponsored prayer service before or after graduation would be improper.

The Court also didn't say anything about students' free speech rights, because free speech was not the issue. The issue is government endorsement of religion. When a school has the right to select its graduation speakers and approve their speeches, that is considered an endorsement of what they say. If the speaker offers a prayer, the school has legally endorsed that prayer.

In Indiana, there has been a lot of media "spin" on the role of the ICLU in all this. We have been accused of threatening school corporations and school children, of placing spies at school graduations and generally contributing to the decline of western civilization.

The truth—inconvenient as it may be—is that a legal foundation funded by Pat Robertson's Christian Coalition sent a "legal memo" to every school board in the United States, urging those boards to include prayer in their graduation ceremonies. The ICLU was deluged with questions from schools that received the memorandum, and because we believed that it was legally and factually wrong, we sent Indiana schools a letter setting out what we believe the law to be.

In our letter, we urged schools to teach students the importance of obeying all laws, not just those with which they may agree. We also pointed out that *intentional* violation of the law would probably lead to a lawsuit against the school corporation and that such suits are costly. (Only a school corporation can violate the First Amendment because only *government* endorsement of religion is unconstitutional.) We concluded our letter by suggesting a constitutionally appropriate alternative to accommodate those who wish to pray: a privately sponsored baccalaureate either immediately before or immediately following the school ceremony. Such a baccalaureate allows those who wish to pray to do so in a meaningful way. Because such a service is private, the prayer need not be "watered down" and generic. Because it is voluntary, it avoids imposing prayer on those whose beliefs may differ. Such a service would appear to accommodate everyone and it is difficult to understand the opposition to this simple alternative.

Would the Republic have crumbled if the Supreme Court had ruled in favor of prayer at graduation? Of course not. Will crime rates rise if students can no longer say a generic prayer during graduation? Of course not. People of good will can differ over the meaning of Supreme Court precedents or the actual intent of the founding fathers as applied to cases like these. But that is not the issue. The issue is whether we will obey the law. It speaks well for Indiana that—despite enormous pressure in some areas of the state—the vast majority of our schools intend to do just that.

We have an opportunity to teach our students two very important lessons: respect for the law, and respect for those who hold opinions different from our own. Those are lessons that can help them build a civil, and civilized, society. How we handle our disputes may ultimately be more important than who won. In a society that respects law, it really *isn't* who wins or loses. It really *is* how we play the game.

Graduation season did finally pass. But it had become obvious to many in both the civil liberties and faith communities that graduation prayer was just one battle in the continuing "culture war"—and that some sort of effort was needed if we were to counter the vitriol unleashed in the name of religion. Accordingly, the ICLU and the Indiana Interreligious Commission on Human Equality, an interfaith organization, convened a Task Force on Religion and the Constitution. Composed primarily of clergy, the group's mission is a modest one: creation of a climate within which we can engage in mutually respectful discussion of issues involving those occasions in which government and religion intersect. As one of the Christian ministers put it, our goal should be to replace "drive-by debate" with genuine dialogue, and to signal the disapproval of faith communities when "the language of religion is used in the service of hate."

Since the public schools have become the focus of

so much acrimony, our first Task Force project was a handbook on religion in the public schools, which we printed and sold through the ICLU. Because we wanted the book to be received in the same spirit in which it was produced (you don't have to hit me over the head twice), we titled it *Less Heat, More Light. Resolving Our Differences in the Communities.* We avoided "legalese" wherever possible, using examples from the Yellow Brick Road Schoolhouse, Foggy Valley School, and other clearly fictional venues to make the law as clear—and nonthreatening—as possible.

The handbook was very basic. We explained why public schools are subject to the First Amendment. (Periodically, there will be a letter to the editor of the local newspaper from someone who has just read the First Amendment for the first time, and has "discovered" that it *only mentions Congress!* Why are we applying it to local schools? Is this some liberal plot? I always want to call the letter writer to suggest further reading. The Fourteenth Amendment imposes upon state governments and their political subdivisions the obligation to respect the rights granted to citizens by the Bill of Rights.) We explained that the Establishment Clause only restrains government, and then only from imposing religious observances or endorsing religious beliefs. Schools can and should teach *about* religion; indeed, it would be impossible to teach history, art, or music without substantial attention to the role of religion. The courts have never, ever suggested that academic attention to religion is improper.

We also explained that the Free Exercise Clause protects individual students from government interference with truly voluntary devotions. A really pernicious falsehood that repeatedly surfaces in these discussions is the charge that "voluntary" prayer has been banished from public school classrooms. Truly voluntary school prayer is absolutely legal; only when prayer is imposed by government does it violate the Establishment Clause. Assuming a student does not suddenly burst into loud devotions in the middle of a math test or otherwise disrupt the learning environment, the school corporation is constitutionally prohibited from interfering. If Johnny bows his head before consuming the lunchroom meatloaf (a prudent precaution in most school cafeterias), the school must respect and accommodate his prayer.

There is a growing mythology to the effect that students all over the country are being punished for such religious expression. A video frequently played on the "700 Club" shows a little girl laboriously climbing into a yellow school bus; she is crippled and the effort is obvious. A voice-over tells us that "Sally" has a long ride to school, and her greatest joy is reading her Bible on the bus—but because of the evil ACLU, it is illegal for her to do so.

The first time I heard this fantasy, I was dumbfounded. The ACLU would go to court in a heartbeat to protect that child's right to read her Bible on the bus. Surely the producers of the very expensive, very slick video know that. Similar tales pop up with regularity. Generally they prove to be equally fictitious. A couple of years ago, I got a call from the national office; a fundraising appeal from a conservative legal foundation had included a report about a school district in Indiana. According to the story, an elementary school teacher had noticed that the face of a young girl's watch featured a picture of Jesus. The teacher reportedly told her that wearing such an item was illegal, due to separation of church and state, and that she would have to remove the watch if she wanted to remain in school. The foundation reportedly had confronted school officials and threatened to sue; only then was the child allowed to return to her classroom. The national office wanted to know if the story was true and if so, why *we* hadn't sued the school. We had heard nothing about the incident, so we called the superintendent. "Yours is the second inquiry I've gotten on that," he told us. "I have no idea where that story came from, but it never happened."

These reports of religious discrimination are generally used to buttress the charge that "separationists" and "secular humanists" hostile to religion are distorting the "real" meaning of religious freedom in their zeal to persecute devout Christians and "drive religion from the public square." I am always bemused by the assertion that religion is being driven out of public life. If by "public life" we mean the common activities of the civic community, a pretty compelling case can be made for the proposition that we have seen a vast *increase* in discussion of religious topics and participation in religious pursuits. Religious radio shows and television networks have proliferated; entire publishing houses and bookstores are devoted to production and sale of religious materials; and I can personally attest to the fact that public debate on religious issues is robust.

Those on the religious right who are concerned with moral issues certainly have a right to contend in the marketplace of ideas; indeed, I believe they have a moral duty to do so. The most fundamental value in our representative democracy is the freedom to express our opinions and attempt to persuade others of the value of those opinions.

When pundits bemoan religion's absence from the "public square," I suspect they really mean the public *sector,* especially the public schools. Proponents of religious exercises in the public schools evidently believe that despite all of the other channels of communication available for religious messages, placing government institutions off-limits amounts to "driving religious influence out of public life." I respectfully disagree.

When we prohibit government from making religious decisions for us, we foster a climate within which our individual faiths can be authentic. We recognize the legitimacy and primacy of the individual conscience and the importance of giving each person the freedom to develop his or her own spirituality. Restraining the state from formalizing and recognizing religion does not marginalize religious belief; to the contrary, it demonstrates profound respect for the integrity of that faith which is chosen freely, without coercion or duress.

Citizens of the United States are no different from our counterparts in Bosnia or Northern Ireland. We do not possess greater tolerance or good will. We have avoided civil strife only because we have constructed and maintained a system of government that respects differences even when a majority of our citizens do not.

Traditional Republicans understand the importance of maintaining that system, of upholding the separation of church and state. Despite the media's preoccupation with the theocratic wing of the party, despite my "prayer wars" with those same folks, their periodic efforts to amend the Constitution to allow school prayer have garnered little enthusiasm from mainstream Republicans. The recent "Religious Freedom" proposal, which would amend the Bill of Rights so that tax dollars could be used to support religious institutions, has likewise languished. In Indiana, in our most recent Republican primary, candidates identified with the Christian Coalition and similar groups fared very poorly overall.

This disinclination to effect a radical change to our Constitutional system is most certainly not hostility to religion. It is recognition of an undeniable fact: Americans are among the most religious people on earth, but we are religious in highly individual ways. We do not diminish the importance of religion by limiting the power of the state to prescribe our prayers. We enhance it.

5

Can We Talk?

★★★

When I was a young girl (admittedly, a long time ago), I was taught that discussions of religion and politics were to be avoided in social gatherings. Since both topics were important and interesting, I thought the rule ridiculous; given the degree of incivility that surrounds discussion of the proper role of religion in our political life these days, I have reconsidered. Certainly, if such discussions are to be useful—if they are truly going to be *discussions*, and not merely an airing of our respective prejudices—we need to infuse them with respect for each other and respect for fact. Respect for both is in short supply.

The media is clearly one source of our collective lack of courtesy. In 1994, when Republicans took control of the House of Representatives, several of them—flush with new power—stated their intent to introduce a constitutional amendment permitting "voluntary" prayer in public school classrooms. I received an invitation to debate the wisdom of such an amendment on a radio call-in show; taking the "pro" position was a minister from a very fundamentalist congregation. I, of course, was to argue against the proposal. The host of the show clearly wanted fireworks; she had invited people with diametrically opposed viewpoints and was undoubtedly anticipating angry exchanges that would generate many calls and drive up ratings.

Unfortunately, from her standpoint, both of us came prepared to listen. The minister was genuinely concerned with the collapse of morality in society. He was not looking for scapegoats, he was looking for solutions. I was certainly willing to concede the validity of many of his concerns; indeed, I shared many of them. Because we were really talking to each other, I was able to explain that the First Amendment already allows truly voluntary prayer, and also to convey my concerns about state-imposed devotions. As a deeply religious person, he did not desire and did not approve of government interference with individual beliefs; his support for a constitutional amendment rested upon a misconception—that such an amendment was the only way to ensure rights that are in fact already guaranteed by the Free Exercise Clause. At the end of the program, while we certainly did not agree on a number of issues, he commented, "Well, if you are correct, and the law really does protect voluntary prayer now, we don't need a constitutional amendment. What we do need is to get together to explain to people what their rights really are." To which I say, "Amen."

The host of the talk show never asked me back. Obviously annoyed that we discussed the issue of prayer in the schools with mutual civility, she interrupted frequently to pose questions intended to be polarizing. When we didn't take the bait and yell at each other, her frustration was evident.

I have frequently thought back to that "debate." It may not have helped the radio station's ratings, but it proved to me that people of good will *can* talk to each other, *can* find common ground to build on in this treacherous and mean-spirited climate. But we need two essential tools: mutual respect and facts.

I cannot count the number of times people have said to me, in all seriousness, that the 1962 decision in *Engle* v. *Vitale,* holding classroom prayer unconstitutional, opened the door to social breakdown. When prayer left the classroom in 1962, according to this theory, guns, drugs, teenage pregnancy, and declining SAT scores came in. Of course, this straightforward cause-and-effect analysis requires us to overlook a fair number of other social and technological changes: the population shift from rural to urban areas; the erosion of the middle class; America's economic restructuring from a manufacturing base to an economy based upon information and services; and profound changes in popular entertainment, which has become both pervasive and explicit in ways never previously seen. And it ignores the fact that SATs are now taken by well over half of high school seniors, rather than the relative elite who took them in the late 1950s and early 1960s.[1] What really dooms this theory, however, is an inconvenient fact: By the time the Supreme Court decided *Engle,* fully 75 percent of all public school districts had already discontinued the practice of state-imposed prayer, mostly under state constitutional provisions (which, interestingly, are often more stringent on the issue of separation than is federal law). Of the remaining 25 percent, it is estimated that fully 40 percent ignored the Court ruling and continued to violate the law for many years. Some still do.

There are a number of other durable myths about

separation of church and state under the First Amendment. Because the literal phrase "separation of church and state" does not appear in the Constitution, radical right publications frequently assert that the concept is a massive fraud perpetrated by liberals, atheists, and (of course) the ACLU. They dismiss the letter Thomas Jefferson wrote to the Danbury (Connecticut) Baptists* in 1802 as a "mere courtesy" and claim that Jefferson's use of the phrase in that letter has been adopted by those who wanted to read a separation theory into the Bill of Rights. In fact, the phrase was used by many of the founders: James Madison, in an 1819 letter, wrote, "the industry and morality of the priesthood and the devotion of the people have been manifestly increased by the total separation of the church and state."[2] Roger Williams, a pioneer of religious liberty and the founder of the Rhode Island colony, had used the phrase at least 150 years earlier. And Jefferson's letter was a major statement on church and state, the text of which was officially reviewed by the attorney general prior to its delivery to the Danbury Baptists.

Periodically, the ICLU receives angry letters (generally unsigned) from self-described religious writers, as-

---

*Jefferson responded to an inquiry about the intent of the First Amendment put to him by the Danbury Baptist Association with the following language: "Believing with you that religion is a matter which lies solely between man and his God; that he owes account to none other for his faith or his worship; that the legislative powers of the government reach actions only, and not opinions—I contemplate with sovereign reverence that act of the whole American people which declared that their legislature should 'make no law respecting an establishment of religion or prohibiting the free exercise thereof' thus building a wall of separation between Church and State." The Danbury Baptists were advocates of freedom of religion, and their inquiry was a formal request for an interpretation.

serting that the United States was established as a
"Christian Nation" and citing as "proof" a Supreme
Court case, *Holy Trinity Church* v. *United States.* I had
never heard of the case before coming to the ICLU, and
I looked it up. In this 1892 decision, written by Justice
David Brewer, there does indeed appear the statement,
"This is a Christian nation." The statement is made in
dicta (what lawyers call comments that are in the nature of "asides"—not a part of the opinion itself), but it
is there. Legal scholars have suggested that what
Brewer meant was that America was composed largely
of citizens who espoused Christianity; however, whatever he may have meant, the case is an anomaly. It has
only been cited as precedent once, and then not for the
proposition that this is a Christian nation. Brewer himself never repeated the statement, or voiced any similar
sentiment, even in cases where he was clearly invited
to do so. Other than this one case, there is no authority
for such a proposition, and a good deal of evidence to
the contrary exists. Luther Martin, a Maryland delegate
to the Constitutional Convention, wanted to distinguish in the Constitution between those who professed
Christianity and those who were "infidels or pagans."
His views were rejected. When George Washington negotiated and signed the Treaty of Tripoli with Turkey in
1797, that document declared that "[T]he Government
of the United States is not, in any sense, founded on
the Christian religion."

By far the most widespread mythology concerns the
meaning of "establishment" of religion. The Religious
Right insists that what was intended was a benign
"nonpreferentialism"—a concern that all religions be
treated equally—and a desire to protect the church
from interference by the state—sort of a one-way wall.
History simply does not bear out either of these claims.

An early draft of the First Amendment that spoke only to the establishment of a national church was rejected; so was a clause that read "Congress shall make no law establishing any particular denomination in preference to another." And there is ample evidence from the writings of Jefferson, Madison, and others to support the current interpretation that the "wall of separation" was intended not only to protect the church from the state, but also to prevent one or more churches from gaining control of the coercive power of the state, to the disadvantage of dissenting beliefs. As Benjamin Franklin wrote in a letter to one Richard Price, "When a religion is good, I conceive that it will support itself; and when it cannot support itself, and God does not take care to support it, so that its professors are obliged to call for the help of the civil power, it is a sign, I apprehend, of its being a bad one."

Those who do not understand the Bill of Rights as a limitation both on government and majority rule get particularly indignant about prayer in classrooms where "the majority" desires it. The notion that America is a democracy, where "the majority" rules is a persistent—and pernicious—misconception. Perhaps the most eloquent response to such misplaced majoritarianism was penned in 1943 by Justice Robert H. Jackson, in *West Virginia State Board of Education* v. *Barnette*. The issue, as he framed it, was whether the Constitution permits the "compulsion of students to declare a belief." In language that has often been quoted, Jackson concluded that

The very purpose of a Bill of Rights was to withdraw certain subjects from the vicissitudes of political controversy, to place them beyond the reach of majorities and officials and to establish them as legal principles to be applied by the courts. One's right to life, liberty, and property, to free speech, a free press, freedom of worship and assembly, and other fundamental rights may not be submitted to a vote; they depend on the outcome of no elections.[3]

We live in an age that celebrates democracy without examining what we mean by that term. Ross Perot's campaign for president touted the desirability of equipping every home with some sort of device that would allow each citizen to vote on each issue, in some version of a town meeting. Our politicians refer daily to polls that are supposed to disclose the desires of their constituents. Our media encourages the notion that elected officials are sent to the legislatures only to do the bidding of the populace, not to exercise independent judgment or be bound by personal conviction. The radical wing of my party cites studies showing that "the people" want prayer in their classrooms as sufficient justification for ignoring the both the Bill of Rights and the most fundamental precepts of the Republican party.

In *The Conscience of a Conservative*, Barry Goldwater lamented that:

> We have gone the way of many a democratic society that has lost its freedom by persuading itself that if "the people" rule, all is well.
>
> The Frenchman, Alexis De Tocqueville, probably the most clairvoyant political observer of modern times, saw the danger when he visited this country in the 1830s. Even then he foresaw decay for a society that tended to put more emphasis on its democracy than on its republicanism. He predicted that America would produce, not tyrants, but "guardians." And that the American people would console themselves for being in tutelage by the reflection that they have chosen their own guardians. Every man allows him-

self to be put in lead-strings, because he sees that it is not a person nor a class of persons but the people at large that hold the end of his chain.[4]

How did the party of Barry Goldwater become identified with a theocratic agenda? How did proponents of principle, of limited government, of genuine religious liberty become identified with religious political extremists who reject these fundamental beliefs?

In 1981, Barry Goldwater addressed the United States Senate on the issue of religious liberty, saying, "We have succeeded for 205 years in keeping the affairs of state separate from the uncompromising idealism of religious groups and we mustn't stop now. To retreat from that separation would violate the principles of conservatism and the values upon which the framers built this democratic republic." In 1995, a mere fourteen years later, David MacIntosh, a freshman Republican in the House of Representatives, wrote this to a constituent:

Ultimately, we must set out an agenda for moral renewal in America. This agenda should, in a loving and tolerant manner, reaffirm moral values in our young people and encourage them to aspire toward virtue. It is vitally important to the future well-being of our country that we undertake such an agenda. Parts of this agenda should be a statute restoring [sic] the power of each community to decide what type of prayer and religious expression they want as part of their public lives. In the Second District of Indiana, we can choose to have prayer in school, while in New York City, they may choose something different.*

---

*This was part of a letter to Mrs. Pat Helms, of Muncie, Indiana, a former Republican precinct committeeperson; she is currently chair of the Muncie chapter of the ICLU.

What has happened to the Republican party between Goldwater and MacIntosh? Aside from the obvious—Goldwater knew his history and MacIntosh doesn't—when did my party begin electing representatives who believe it is their job to determine *my* moral agenda? Why does my party characterize as "rising stars" those like MacIntosh who are willing to use the power of government (in a "loving and tolerant" manner, to be sure) to compel our prayers?

As I wrote to Representative MacIntosh, "As a lifelong Republican, I am most concerned by your willingness to use the power of government to compel behavior you believe to be desirable. Advocates of limited government, of whom I am one, cannot have it both ways. Either individual citizens have moral and economic authority over their own lives, or they don't. Just as one cannot be 'a little bit pregnant' one cannot be selectively totalitarian."

I did not receive any answer, and I really did not expect one; unlike the minister with whom I had the productive radio debate, those on the front lines of the assault on our freedoms are not interested in dialogue. They are not looking for common ground, or for mutual understanding, and they are contemptuous of fact. They have no interest in talking, or even acknowledging that others are entitled to participate in the discussion. They have captured a political power base, and they intend to use it in a manner which I find neither "loving" nor "tolerant."

NOTES

1. See *Our Constitutional Heritage*, ACLU video, 1995.

2. Quoted in Robert S. Alley, ed. *James Madison on Religious Liberty* (Amherst, N.Y.: Prometheus Books, 1985).

3. *West Virginia State Board of Education* v. *Barnette*, 319 U.S. 624 (1943).

4. Barry Goldwater, *The Conscience of a Conservative* (Shepherdsville, Ky.: Victor Publishing, 1960).

6

Death and Taxes

★★

One of the greatest strengths of the ACLU is also one of its greatest weaknesses: We are not seen as a single-issue organization.

On the positive side of the ledger, this means that we appeal to a number of different constituencies. Perhaps you don't care about reproductive choice but efforts to censor the Internet drive you crazy. We're still your organization. Furthermore, single-issue organizations live or die financially based upon the perceived threat to the one issue they champion. (Just ask Planned Parenthood what happened to fundraising immediately after Clinton was elected. Prochoice donors assumed that reproductive freedom was safe under a Democratic administration, and giving declined precipitously.)

On the negative side, whenever an organization takes a position on an issue, it offends those who disagree with that position. More positions, more likelihood of giving offense. I cannot count the number of times I have discussed the ACLU with Republican friends, only to discover that they agree with 95 percent of our positions, but are so firmly opposed to the remaining 5 percent that it colors their perception of the entire organization.

There is another, more serious problem with the perception of the ACLU as a multi-issue organization. The perception itself is wrong. In a very real sense, we are the ultimate single-issue advocacy group, and failure to understand that fact is failure to understand the ACLU. The problem is in defining our issue so that it can be clearly seen as the unifying (and libertarian) principle it is.

A devotion to civil liberties is really belief in a fundamental premise: Government action is subject to restraint. Might does not make right; the ends do not justify the means. Those who crafted our legal system understood what partisans of both left and right frequently forget—the government that can impose my agenda today can impose someone else's tomorrow. No matter how convinced I may be that I am acting for the greater good by suppressing a "dirty" book, preventing a hateful Ku Klux Klan rally, outlawing "cult" religions, or gouging one taxpayer to benefit another, what I am *really* doing is using the power of the state to further my own ends. The alternative to the principle that government must "play by the rules," is the triumph of raw power.

The nation's founders had seen power abused. The weakness of central authority under the Articles of Confederation was intentional; it was a reaction to their very real concern that concentrations of power lead more or less inevitably to despotism. A democratic mandate was not considered sufficient restraint; Madison, Jefferson, and company were keenly aware that the tyranny of one's neighbors, the despotism of popular passion, is not inherently superior to the autocracy of the crown. When it became obvious that a workable central government required more authority than the Articles of Confederation had allowed, they took great care to limit the reach of the additional powers granted by the new Constitution. The arguments over the necessity for a Bill of Rights were not disputes over the need to rein in government power; on that, most Federalists and Antifederalists agreed. The dispute was between those who thought the Constitution clear in permitting government *only* the powers explicitly granted and who felt that the proposed amendments would be superfluous at best and mischievous at worst; and those who were concerned that without a further enumeration of rights specifically reserved to the states and individuals, government would inevitably infringe on the fundamental liberties of its citizens.

The single theme that unifies ACLU positions on a wide variety of issues is our insistence upon adherence to these limits on the power of the state. If this seems an oversimplification, let's look at the ICLU's approach to death and taxes, among other matters that might seem at first glance to be unrelated.

In 1991, the ICLU became involved as *amici* (friend of the court) in the case *In re: Lawrance.* The facts were not in dispute; Sue Ann Lawrance was one of five children born to William and Bonita Lawrance. He is a dentist, she a nurse. By all accounts, they had a loving and happy family life. When Sue Ann was nine, she sustained brain damage in a bicycle accident. Her parents continued to care for her at home for many years; however, when a series of seizures left her unable to function, they placed her in a nursing home. Family members visited regularly, but Sue Ann slipped into a persistent vegetative state. While not technically brain dead, doctors gently informed the family that—barring a miracle—Sue Ann would never regain consciousness. Unwilling to accept that inevitability, the family kept Sue Ann "alive" for the next four years with intravenous nutrition and hydration. Finally, the Lawrance family faced up to a situation that most of us hope never to confront. After anguished consultation with their pastor, and discussions that involved Sue Ann's siblings, other family members, and the doctors who had been treating her, they decided to discontinue the artificial feeding and let Sue Ann go. Because the law governing termination of such life support was unclear in Indiana, the nursing home's attorneys asked a court to review the decision to insure that it had been made with due regard for Sue Ann's rights. No one anticipated a problem, but everyone involved wanted to do the right thing.

Then the unanticipated occurred. Representatives of a group presenting themselves as friends of the disabled filed a petition to be named Sue Ann's guardian. They gave interviews to the media, decrying her imminent "murder." They demanded that the courts reject the family's petition, and called upon the legislature to enact measures that would prevent families from "disposing" of relatives who had become "inconvenient." None of Sue Ann's self-described defenders had ever met her, nor had they had any prior contact with the family. As Sue Ann's sister-in-law Jan was to remark later, none of them had ever emptied a bedpan, or sat by her unresponsive bed, or conferred with her doctors, or cried into their pillows at night.

The case went all the way to the Indiana Supreme Court, which ruled that medical decisions affecting incompetents who had not left contrary instructions in a living will or durable power of attorney were properly made by the families of those incompetents. During the litigation, Sue Ann had died, but the battle wasn't over. During the next three legislative sessions, living will legislation was the focus of emotional arguments; should persons making such wills be allowed to include instructions about artificial nutrition and hydration? The right-to-life advocates who had lost the battle to have government dictate the medical treatment of incompetents now were arguing that it should be illegal for a *competent* adult to rule out extraordinary life support measures.

Who decides how you will end your days? Do we require the state to respect an individual's decisions, or do we allow government to override that individual's wishes? If I instruct my children that I do not wish my life artificially prolonged (as I have), if I reduce those instructions to a writing, properly drafted and attested to, do I not have a fundamental right to expect my wishes to be honored? The state may legitimately assert an interest in verifying that I was not coerced into my decision, but it has no interest that would justify overruling it. Ultimately, the Indiana legislature agreed. Republican legislators split on the issue, with the libertarian wing of the party favoring individual autonomy and the authoritarian wing insisting upon government's right to decide how each of us shall die.

Death and taxes. Recently, the ICLU brought a lawsuit alleging that Indiana's method of assessing property for tax purposes is unconstitutional. We assert that the current method violates the equal protection and due process guarantees of the Bill of Rights, as well as a provision of the state constitution requiring uniformity in the treatment of taxpayers.

Indiana is one of only two states in the country—Nevada is the other—that values property without reference to its market value. Instead, local assessors apply a cumbersome formula known as "Regulation 17" in order to calculate the "true tax value" of property. The "true tax value" is then multiplied by the relevant rate in order to arrive at the tax which is payable. Because the state has 1,008 separate townships, each with its own assessor, and because the formula is imprecise and highly subjective, taxpayers owning property of identical market value have received dramatically differing assessments.

When we announced this lawsuit, people expressed surprise. What does property tax have to do with civil liberties? Although the suit has to rank among our most popular—everyone has property tax horror stories in Indiana—it also demonstrated once again that the organization's mission is not understood. The issue is not the fairness of Indiana's tax system, although the system will undoubtedly be fairer if we win. The issue is whether government can ignore the rule that says each of us is entitled to equality before the law. Similarly situated taxpayers are entitled to be treated similarly.

Every position the ICLU adopts, every case we take, involves a threshold analysis of the role played by government. Many members of the ICLU oppose abortion but believe passionately that the government has no business making reproductive decisions for individual women. We oppose censorship efforts of both left and right—crusaders for "family values" on the one hand and those who would impose "politically correct" speech codes or limits on "hate speech" on the other—because it is not the business of government to decide what we read or say. We support religious freedom, because government ought not have the power to compel our devotions. The ACLU opposed the second trial of the police officers who beat Rodney King* (although virtually all of us felt that the first trial had been a miscarriage of justice) because government ought not have the power to try people over and over for the same crime.

Local Republicans were delighted when the ICLU sued the administration of our Democratic governor for improperly firing employees of the Bureau of Motor Vehicles. The fired driving examiners were all Republican; their replacements all Democrats. We would have sued a Republican governor had he done the same to Democratic employees, because government ought not be able to fire nonpolicy makers for holding the "wrong" political beliefs. It's the libertarian principle of the thing.

In all fairness, it isn't easy to be principled about the things we care about most. There is a part of each of us that knows best what is good for everyone else, and is impatient when constitutional "technicalities" intrude. When I have discussions with my Republican friends who say they agree with the ACLU about some things but not others, I tell them that one cannot be selectively totalitarian. As tempting as it sometimes is, once we decide that it is okay for the state to break the rules just this once in order to achieve a greater good, we are no longer applying principle. We are exercising power. Worse, we are creating a justification for the next departure from principle, and the next.

People do not really agree or disagree with the ACLU on discrete issues, because at bottom, there is only one issue: the power of government.

---

*Rodney King was a black motorist whose savage beating by the Los Angeles police was captured on videotape in 1991. The state trial of the officers involved ended with an acquittal that sparked widespread rioting in south central L.A. Two police officers were subsequently convicted in a federal court proceeding in which they were charged with violating King's civil rights.

When people say that they agree with the ACLU about some things but not about others, what they are really saying is that they are willing to apply the libertarian principle selectively. They are saying they believe in limiting the power of the state when the state is doing something with which they disagree, but are willing to employ that power in furtherance of goals of which they approve. They are endorsing the notion that the ends justify the means.

7

Purveyors of Filth
at the Local Library

★★★

Nat Hentoff* once wrote that the human animal's desire to censor is stronger than even our sex drive. I
think he may be right.

Recently, across the country, those concerned with
declining "family values" have settled on an unlikely
target—public libraries. When I was raising my children,
I operated under the theory that kids who hung out at
the local Carnegie were probably not the ones I should
be worried about. This attitude evidently makes me a
very bad parent in the eyes of our local "God squad."

Locally, the conflict began a year or so ago, when a
small group of parents demanded that the Indianapolis
public library restrict certain videos accessible to minors unless the child's borrowing had been expressly

---

*Hentoff is a columnist for the *Village Voice* newspaper and author of several books, including *American Heroes: In and Out of
School* (New York: Delacorte Press, 1987).

authorized by the parent. The library board declined, but in an effort to accommodate those who had expressed concern, agreed to place restrictions on the library card of any child whose parent requested it. This seemed to me to be a very reasonable approach; it allowed individual parents to determine what their children should see without empowering government to make a preliminary determination of suitability from which the parent must appeal.

Over half a million people have library cards in our county; in the first six months the new policy was in effect (and heavily publicized), only thirty-nine parents took advantage of the library's offer.

To the original petitioners, this lack of interest simply confirmed the extent of moral rot in our society. Clearly, stronger measures were required. *All* videos should be off-limits to minors unless their parents specifically permitted viewing. When additional appeals to the library board met with resistance, the parents went to the City Council. (The council has no direct jurisdiction over the libraries, but it does appoint members of the library board; a vote against current library policy would thus be seen as cautionary by those board members desiring to be reappointed.)

Arguments flew back and forth. Librarians were accused of having "deviant lifestyles." In a library hearing, when I suggested to an emotional mother that as parents we ought to be responsible for our own children, she responded angrily, "What if *your* child takes out a video and shows it to *my* child?" Those who were appalled by this attempt to prescribe what other people's children should see spoke of censorship; those who favored the restrictions spoke of "protecting children." It is hard to be against protecting children.

Predictably, the council committee endorsed the

nonbinding resolution, despite a hearing at which—to my surprise and gratitude—public opposition was virtually unanimous, and a number of prominent local Republicans testified against the proposal. (Like me, most of the Republicans in opposition were from the "old guard," the Republican mainstream.) After a long procession of people had addressed the committee, many defending their right as parents to determine what their children should see, an angry councilwoman took the microphone to ask "Is everyone here a library member? Will everyone who has a library card stand up?" Apparently, the opinions of those who actually *used* the library were to be discounted. Beulah Coughenour—the same council member who had sponsored the infamous Dworkin/MacKinnon pornography ordinance in order to "protect" women—testified that government must protect all those children at the library who do not have "good" parents. (She did not define "good.") Every single council member who voted for the proposal prefaced his or her vote with a statement denying that censorship was involved.

Contemporary culture warriors (too many of whom are Republicans or in Congress or both) tell us we must restrict expression in order to promote morality. We traditional Republicans who believe in the importance of limited government and free speech will make a huge mistake if we concede the moral high ground to these people, because liberty and self-government are themselves profoundly *moral* values. The marketplace of ideas is an absolutely essential condition of our public morality; it reflects the conviction that neither civic nor personal virtue is possible without free choice.

Man's freedom to search for truth was of paramount importance in the philosophies of those who fashioned the American nation; it was an article of faith that truth cannot be known unless *all* ideas are available for examination.

The founders also believed that only an informed citizenry could be entrusted with self-government. As Alexander Meiklejohn, a respected American philosopher, once wrote:

> When men govern themselves, it is they—and no one else—who must pass judgment upon unwisdom and unfairness and danger. And that means that unwise ideas must have a hearing as well as wise ones, unfair as well as fair, dangerous as well as safe, unAmerican as well as American. Just so far as, at any point, the citizens who are to decide an issue are denied acquaintance with information or opinion or doubt or disbelief or criticism which is relevant to that issue, just so far the result must be ill-considered, ill-balanced planning for the general good. *It is the mutilation of the thinking process of the community against which the First Amendment to the Constitution is directed.* . . . To be afraid of ideas, any idea, is to be unfit for self-government. [Emphasis in original.][1]

It was not just that the founders considered access to all ideas essential. They also understood that liberty is an all-or-nothing proposition. When authorities can pick and choose which ideas are acceptable, no ideas are safe.

Not long after I moved to the ICLU, my husband and I had a small dinner party. Among the guests was a friend with whom I had worked on several political campaigns and her husband, who is also an active Republican. They are not only good citizens, they are both good people, in the very best sense of the word: honorable, caring, modest, and open-minded. After dinner, talk turned to the ICLU and its mission; the wife promised to come into the office from time to time to help manage volunteers. The husband, who had been looking increasingly uncomfortable, asked if he could talk to me alone for a moment. We went into the next room. "I understand limiting government," he told me. "But how can you defend some of the filth that is out there? Have you listened to the lyrics of some of this rap music? Do you know there is one called 'Cop Killer'?" I tried to explain to him that the government that can ban "Cop Killer" can also decide that Shakespeare's exhortation to "kill all the lawyers" should be excised from his play;[2] that the issue is not the value of the expression, but the authority to decide its value. I don't think I got very far. Of the two dangers he saw— bad speech versus big government—bad speech seemed to him the greater evil.

From the very beginning, America did not live up to the ideal of a truly free marketplace of ideas. First were the Alien and Sedition Acts,* then attempts to stamp out obscenity, then efforts to ban books that someone found offensive. At one time or another, Americans have banned *Tarzan, Little Red Riding Hood,* the *Diary of Anne Frank, Huckleberry Finn,* and even the dictionary. Once television was invented, there was a whole new threat; people like the Rev. Donald Wildmon† want to ban MTV and a number of prime-time shows which they believe are immoral. Congress continues to insist

---

*The Alien and Sedition Acts were early attempts to declare certain speech "seditious," likely to cause an uprising, and to ban it as a danger to the republic.

†Donald Wildmon founded and runs the American Family Association, an ultraconservative organization that began by criticizing popular culture and calling for movies and television to be cleaned up. The group has changed its focus to step up its criticism on the separation of church and state.

that "indecency" be removed from radio, television, and the Internet.

All of these efforts miss the point. In our system, the issue is *not* what is said. The merit, worth, correctness, or morality of any particular expression is constitutionally irrelevant. The question is who decides what is said? Who decides which ideas are worth transmitting and which are not?

Censors always justify themselves by promising to protect us only from expression that is "dangerous" or "immoral." Talk of treason will lead people to overthrow the government. Rock music will produce sexual abandon. Hate speech will cause violence. There is some truth to each of these assertions; if ideas weren't powerful, if they didn't matter, they wouldn't be worth protecting. But in our system the way to counter bad ideas is with good ideas. Put another way, it is better— and safer—to bleach garbage in the sunlight than to allow it to fester and smell in the dark. The corollary is that each of us, in a free country, is responsible for generating some of the sunlight.

The censor doesn't want to bother arguing against an idea. He does not trust the public to reject that which has no value, or is tasteless, or wrong. He wants to make that decision for us. It can be tempting to turn over our personal responsibility, to let government do it. Freedom is a lot of work.

I must admit I sometimes get impatient with those who are unwilling to exercise the responsibilities of citizenship, those I call "moral couch potatoes." A year or so ago, I got a call at the ICLU office from a man who began the conversation by saying he had seen me on television and he knew that "you people don't believe in censorship." Nevertheless, he proceeded to inform me that his neighborhood video store had on its shelves a video that was "absolutely vile." He paused for breath, and I couldn't help myself. I lit into him. "If this video is so awful, what are you doing about it?" There was utter silence. "Have you told the store owner you disapprove?" He had not. "Have you written the producer?" He had not. "Have you and your neighbors picketed?" They had not. In fact, he had done absolutely nothing to counter what he perceived to be pernicious ideas except to demand that someone else—in this case, the government—do it for him. Sorry, but as I told him, that is just not the American way.

Noted science fiction author Robert Silverberg is said to have begun a speech at a science-fiction convention by saying, "Ninety percent of science fiction is crap. But then, 90 percent of everything is crap." The issue is not the value of the particular speech that is targeted; the issue is our right—indeed, our obligation—to determine for ourselves what is wheat and what is chaff. In a free country, different people will reach different conclusions; if that were not the case, censors wouldn't be wanted. If there were to be general agreement about what is offensive, no one would buy the book, see the movie, rent the video, or download the information. By definition, the only time people ask government to step in is when one group wants to restrict what another group wants to see.

These thoughts of prominent Christian theologian C. S. Lewis were once posted on the Internet:

Of all tyrannies, a tyranny exercised for the good of its victims may be the most oppressive. It may be better to live under robber barons than under omnipotent moral busybodies. The robber baron's cruelty may sometimes sleep, his cupidity may at some point be satiated; but those who torment us for our

own good will torment us without end, for they do so
with the approval of their consciences.

Ironically, just a couple of years ago, in a small town
in southern Indiana, Lewis himself became the target of
such busybodies. A school corporation had instituted
an entirely voluntary program to encourage elementary
students to read. A group of parents from a local fundamentalist church demanded that the school board discontinue the program because the books on the list
were "anti-Christian." One of the objectionable works
was Lewis's *The Lion, the Witch and the Wardrobe*, a
moral parable which has delighted children and educators for years. (One wonders if these agitated parents
ever *read* the books they denounce. Or is the mere reference to witches in the title sufficient to confirm that
the book is an apologia for witchcraft and other "New
Age" blasphemies?) Once again, it was no defense that
the program was voluntary, and that a child's participation was entirely up to that child's parents. The "anti-
Christian" influences would harm the entire community. The school board capitulated and a much-praised
program was discontinued. Parents who wanted their
children to participate were just out of luck.

If "anti-Christian" is in the eye of the beholder, so are
"obscenity" and "pornography," the censor's most
common targets. Even those who believe that hard-core
obscenity is not protected by the First Amendment will
concede that the government has frequently stretched
the definition in order to suppress speech that clearly is
protected; it wasn't all that long ago when those dis-
seminating birth control information were subjected to
prosecution under so-called obscenity laws.

What is "pornographic" (a more elastic term than
obscenity, which does at least have a legal definition)

depends almost entirely upon the perspective of the viewer. The Rev. Donald Wildmon says the mission of his organization, the American Family Association, is to rid the American media, particularly television, of "soft and hard pornography." In the organization's literature he defines such pornography as "not dirty words and dirty pictures. It is a philosophy of life which seeks to remove the influence of Christians and Christianity from our society." The American Family Association has campaigned against such television programs as "Cheers," "Alf," "Nightline," "60 Minutes," and many other shows that most of us would not consider remotely "pornographic."

In December 1995, Wildmon used his American Family Association's Internet site to transmit the following message:

> Once again, it is time for us to stand up and tell the liberal entertainment industry that America will not tolerate the continual erosion of the minds of our young people with obscene pornography disguised as "family entertainment."
>
> The Walt Disney Company, one of America's leading distributors of lucrative, mind-rotting garbage aimed at children—*The Lion King, Aladdin*—is at it again. *Toy Story,* the company's big Christmas release, is positively the most disgusting example of Hollywood's use of pornography to line its coffers since ABC-TV's "NYPD Blue."
>
> Some of the following descriptions may be offensive, so please keep this out of the hands of your children:
>
> In *Toy Story,* rated G by the ultra-liberal MPAA, the main characters, "Woody"—note sexual reference—and "Buzz"—note drug reference—are owned by a child in a single-parent household in which the father is noticeably absent. "Woody" and "Buzz" have

equally disturbing toy friends, including a sex-obsessed talking potato, a sex-obsessed Bo Peep doll
who cannot keep her hands (or lips) off "Woody" and
an Etch-a-Sketch whose "knobs" must be "adjusted"
to produce results.

* * * * * * * * * * * * *

Please write or call the creators and distributors of
this filth and let them know that you are *fed up* with
their reckless and immoral actions. AFA efforts like
this are keeping pornography off store shelves, off
television sets, and out of theaters and video stores of
America, but *we must not let up.* As long as Hollywood
does not get the message and *wake up,* we must continue to tell them how America feels.[3]

This transmittal reminds me of the old story of the
man whose psychiatrist was conducting an evaluation.
During the ink-blot test, he showed the patient a
number of ink-blots and asked him what he saw. Each
time, the patient responded with a sexual image; he saw
intercourse in one blot, a naked woman in another, and
so forth. At the end of the test, the psychiatrist said,
"You know, you really have a problem." *"Me?"* said the
man. *"You're* the one showing all the dirty pictures!"

In September 1995, Sens. Orrin Hatch (R-Utah),
Charles Grassley (R-Iowa), Spencer Abraham (R-Mich.),
and Strom Thurmond (R-S.C.) introduced a bill in Congress to expand the scope of federal "child pornography" laws. Billed as an effort to "protect" children, it
would criminalize images of fully clothed children if the
setting of the photograph is considered "sexually sug-
gestive." Considered by whom? Reverend Wildmon? Pat
Robertson? Or Hugh Hefner? Put away those old family
photos of the baby on the bearskin rug!

I have no doubt that many of these efforts at censorship are well-intentioned; as C. S. Lewis reminds us, however, that does not make them any less dangerous. There simply is no general agreement on what constitutes "pornography" and it is highly doubtful that such agreement is even possible. As ACLU President Nadine Strossen puts it: "If it turns me on, it's erotica. If it turns *you* on, it's pornography."[4]

As often as civil libertarians emphasize that the issue is liberty—that although we do not necessarily approve of what you choose to read or view, we do believe that you have the right to make your own decisions—it is a distinction that many people simply cannot seem to understand. During the lawsuit over the Indianapolis pornography ordinance, I was flown to Washington, D.C., for a late-night call-in television show. Andrea Dworkin, one of the original authors of the measure, was the other guest. She spoke of women's blood running in the streets; I spoke (rather primly, as I recall) about constitutional rights and the First Amendment. I emphasized the overbreadth of the ordinance, the fact that it would endanger much more than the sorts of materials its proponents described; she talked about women being raped and dismembered. At the end of the program, a call came in from a man who identified himself as a New Jersey fireman. He said that he and his buddies had been watching the show, and he couldn't figure out "why Mrs. Kennedy, who seems like such a nice woman, is *for* pornography?"

Some days, it just doesn't pay to get up.

While there are as many would-be censors on the left as on the right, it is undeniable that the loudest voices today urging government to "protect morality" are those who call themselves conservative. I would recommend to them the following passages from *The Conscience of a Conservative*:

> The founding fathers had a *reason* for endorsing the principle of limited government; and this reason recommends defense of the constitutional scheme even to those who take their citizenship obligations lightly. The reason is simple, and it lies at the heart of the Conservative philosophy.
>
> Throughout history, government has proved to be the chief instrument for thwarting man's liberty. Government represents power in the hands of some men to control and regulate the lives of other men. And power, as Lord Acton said, *corrupts* men. "Absolute power," he added, "corrupts absolutely."[5]

Republicans should be the *last* people to turn over to government the power to decide what books we may read, what movies we may see, or what ideas we may consider.

NOTES

1. A. Meiklejohn, *Free Speech in Its Relation to Self-Government* (Port Washington, N.Y.: Kennikat Press, 1948).

2. William Shakespeare, *Henry VI, Part 2*, act 4, sc. 2.

3. American Family Association Website (originally <http://gocin.com/afa/home.htm>, the current address of this site is <http://www.afa.net>), December 5, 1995, List AFA-L, subject: Boycott *Toy Story*.

4. Speech by Nadine Strossen, Indianapolis, Indiana, March 1995.

5. Barry Goldwater, *The Conscience of a Conservative* (Shepherdsville, Ky.: Victor Publishing, 1960), pp. 16–17.

8

A Day at the General Assembly, or What If These People Really Are Representative?

★★

For someone who has been political all my adult life, when I came to work at the ICLU, I was shamefully ignorant of the legislative process. I was okay in the abstract—I knew how a bill became a law. I even had a degree of what some call cynicism but I prefer to think of as realism: the knowledge that every vote cast by an elected representative is not carefully weighed on its merits; that concern for one's own political and even economic advantage are an inescapable part of the legislative process at every level. But because my experience with political people had been largely positive, I had an expectation that most legislators would be thoughtful and—within the limits of political ideology and self-interest—committed to providing good government. Many are. But an appalling number confirm a remark made to me years ago by the wife of a powerful Indiana House member: "Just remember," she said darkly, "the legislature is a *representative* body." She was right. Our legislators represent the entire spectrum of our society—educated and uneducated, openminded and bigoted, kind and meanspirited, quick and slow.

Not long after I became executive director, we were able to attract a young intern whom we later hired to be my Associate Director for Legislation and Education. She was young, very bright, and absolutely committed to civil liberties; her major in college had been Constitutional Studies. For reasons I have yet to comprehend, Terri thoroughly enjoys doing battle at the legislature. The ICLU has also been incredibly lucky to have had a long-time vice-president for legislation who is both knowledgeable about the process and an expert on civil liberties; however, she does not live in the capital and cannot be at the legislature every day it is in session. The employment of a lobbyist had been a long-time goal. Together, the two of them follow the hundreds of bills proposed and the arcane process by which those proposals are heard and voted on. I do not envy them.

Two anecdotes—both true—may suggest what we are up against. During the last session, Terri was running late for a committee hearing on a bill we were following. As she entered the hearing room and slid into an empty seat, one of the legislators on the committee turned to another, and in a whisper audible to the entire room, said, "There's the ICLU with that damn Constitution again!" During another hearing, a state representative suggested that a measure under consideration might violate the First Amendment's free speech provisions. He was asked what the First Amendment said, and replied that he was unsure. When no one on the committee or the committee staff was able to recall what the First Amendment said, they sent a page to obtain a copy.

Every person we elect to make our laws takes an oath

to uphold the constitutions of Indiana and the United States. Is it too much to ask that they at least *read* them?

Discussion with my colleagues in the ACLU suggests that our experience in Indiana mirrors a national phenomenon. Even a cursory look at the national news confirms that Congress is no exception.

American political history provides plenty of evidence that we have always elected a smattering of buffoons and loose cannons. We have always had negative campaigns (when Thomas Jefferson ran for president, opponents charged that he would burn the Bible and decree atheism across the land). Partisanship is not new. And this is hardly the first generation to hold the political enterprise in contempt. Are legislators and legislative bodies really any worse today than they have ever been? And if so, how and why?

I have reluctantly concluded that today's situation is, indeed, worse. Congress and statehouses all across the country have become increasingly polarized and mean-spirited. Our representatives are disdainful of nuance and complexity, preferring to substitute slogans for solutions and sound bytes for analyses. Ronald Reagan used to be criticized for oversimplifying; much of the time, I found that criticism unfair, because he tended to talk about *principles*. Principles are simple; application of those principles to existing problems is rarely so. Those of us who defend the libertarian principle sometimes explain it thusly: You may swing your fist until it comes in contact with my nose. In other words, individuals may enjoy the maximum liberty compatible with an absence of social harm. Simple. Except there are as many definitions of social harm as there are people on the planet. You have a right to smoke a cigarette, but do you have a right to fill my environment with passive smoke? You have a right to drive a motorcycle, but does that include a right to drive up the cost of automobile insurance for those who drive safe little sedans and never fail to buckle up? What if I am convinced that your "art" is a pollution of the culture that undermines the quality of life for everyone? Suddenly, what was simple no longer is quite so straightforward. Our current crop of lawmakers seems incapable of understanding the distinction between "simple" principle and its application to a far more complex reality.

When Americans still understood the difference between representative democracy and pure democracy, we tended to elect as our representatives those we considered to be the "best and brightest." Those who asked for our votes were likely to stress personal qualities like judgment and educational background—qualities that presumably equipped them to make informed and principled decisions on our behalf. Implicit in these campaigns was the issue of trustworthiness—not "Do you trust the candidate to be faithful to his or her spouse?" but "Do you trust this candidate to study the issues, understand and weigh the interests involved, and make a decision consistent with what he or she believes to be the good?" When I first became involved in politics, the term "statesman" did not sound quaint. I cannot recall the last time I heard an officeholder referred to as a "public servant" rather than as a politician. The language reflects our perception of current reality.

What has brought the political enterprise to this pass? Social scientists can argue over the causes, but it is indisputable that three features of today's political landscape play a large role. The first, and most obvious, is the media. It is fashionable to talk about the "inside the beltway" mentality of Congress, and ultraconservatives like Rush Limbaugh bemoan how cut off our representatives are from "real" citizens. In fact, isolation is impossible. The media is more omnipresent, more instantaneous, more intrusive than our forebears could have imagined. Any citizen who is interested in Congress can turn on C-SPAN and watch gavel to gavel coverage; an explosion of magazines and newsletters follow events in the nation's capital and state capitals, radio talk show hosts spend hours inviting the (frequently uninformed) views of voters, and the Internet provides millions of bytes of information *and* an instantaneous mechanism for registering citizens' opinions. For those unconnected to the Internet but unwilling to trust the postal service, fax machines offer another avenue for citizen feedback. Reporters and pundits concentrate on how well the elected one is representing the desires of his or her constituency; and I seriously doubt that many of the communiqués arriving via Internet, fax, or postcard are urging our representatives to think the issue over carefully and vote their own consciences. From a hundred directions, elected officials are subjected to unrelenting scrutiny with a single message: You have been sent to the legislature to reflect popular opinion and nothing more.

There is another effect directly attributable to the pervasiveness of the media: a sound-byte mentality. In an era of intense competition for readers and viewers, the media must attract and serve a market, and that frequently means KISS—keep it simple, stupid. If it won't fit in a headline or on a bumper sticker; if there isn't a "hook" to the story, it is unlikely to get much attention from the mainstream media. There is no reward for the legislator who genuinely understands a complex issue and wants to convey those complexities to the public.

The second influence simply reinforces the first. If we elect people to reflect majoritarian passions, then it is very important to know what those passions are, and whether they have changed since yesterday. Polls give our politicians access to that data. They are anything but perfect; any pollster will readily list the limitations—how the questions are framed, how the demographics are constructed, can dramatically affect results. But political figures ignore them at their peril. I once suggested to a local legislator that we might perfect polling sufficiently to allow us to dispense with elected representatives altogether. After all, if his sole duty was to reflect popular will, he could be replaced by a really valid poll taker. He wasn't amused—but he wasn't embarrassed either, and I thought he should be.

The third reason our politics are so poisonous today is our increased ability to gerrymander. (A good friend of mine, a former state senator with a passion for political history, shared this analysis with me; I was struck by its logic—and frightened by its implications.) Gerrymandering, or the drawing of election districts for political advantage, is as old as the nation. Both parties engage in the practice. The party that controls the state legislature at redistricting time draws the lines— for the city council, the state legislature, and Congress. Those in control proceed to create the maximum possible number of "safe" districts. For their own party, the object is to produce as many seats as possible while still maintaining a comfortable majority of dependable party voters in each. After that, the object is to cram as many of the other party's voters as possible into as few districts as possible. This process leaves relatively few political subdivisions where the parties are genuinely engaged, and either one can reasonably hope to win based upon the candidates and the issues rather than the political affiliation of the voters. In the past, it was difficult to get all the information needed to gerrymander with assurance; in an era of computers, the accuracy with which safe districts can be drawn has increased exponentially.

The genius of the American system, and the source of much of its stability, has always been the pressure to move toward the political middle. Recurring complaints about the two major parties, to the effect that they are "Tweedle Dee" and "Tweedle Dum," obscured the very real benefit of the large overlap between them. Unlike many European parliamentary systems, our political structure tends toward the center, toward the kind of consensus that ultimately makes governing possible. We elect Republicans and move somewhat to the right; Democrats, and move somewhat to the left. As the location of the political center changes, so does our notion of what constitutes "somewhat." The result is that change occurs incrementally over time, and with less dislocation than might otherwise be the case. Sophisticated gerrymandering is changing that.

In a safe legislative district, the real election occurs in the primary. Since the general election has been foreordained, the candidates look only to the party faithful when shaping their positions. Primary voters, in both parties, are more ideological than voters in general elections. As a result, safe districts elect candidates who are more extreme than those elected by voters in districts that are truly "in play." The Republican incumbent in a safe district watches his right flank; the Democrat in a safe seat watches his left. Neither has any incentive to move to the middle in order to win the general election. Congress and state legislatures end up filled with ideologues who see no need to compromise (and possible electoral retribution if they do so).

The result of these influences—an omnipresent media, continuous polling, and ever-more-precise gerrymandering—is a legislative process that bears little resemblance to the representative and deliberative mechanism intended by the founders. Madison believed that representative government would "refine and enlarge the public views by passing them through the medium of a chosen body of citizens." Hamilton predicted that Congress "with too few exceptions to have any influence on the spirit of the government, will be composed of landholders, merchants, and men of the learned professions."[1]

It bears emphasizing that the problem today is not gridlock—at least, not as the term is popularly understood. Public impatience with representatives who don't move quickly enough to address issues is generally misplaced. Our system was intentionally built to include gridlock, what the founders called necessary checks and balances. As Madison put it, government should be so constructed "that its several constituent parts may, by their mutual relations, be the means of keeping each other in their proper places." The problem is the *reason* for today's version of gridlock: unreflective partisanship, the conviction that compromise equals defeat; and a loss of even the most elementary generosity of spirit or civility.

As this book is being written, an unprecedented number of Congresspersons are voluntarily leaving government. Virtually every one of them has cited the loss of civility and the inability to work across party lines in a spirit of compromise and collegiality as the reason for departure.

Whatever one may think of any particular element of the Republican "Contract with America," introduced by Newt Gingrich* and Republican candidates for the

---

*Gingrich, a Georgia Republican, was elected Speaker of the U.S. House of Representatives in 1995 and reelected in 1997.

U.S. House of Representatives in the 1994 elections, the concept was consistent with the original idea of representation. By casting a political platform in the form of a proposed contract with constituents, Republican candidates showed respect for the historic distinction between direct and representative democracy. They asked us to elect them based upon their stated positions and objectives, and to delegate to them the job of actually creating laws consistent with those positions. Implicit in the contract approach is our right as voters to evaluate their performance against their positions and to cast our votes elsewhere if we are displeased. So far, so good.

Unfortunately, many of those who were elected did not interpret the contract as I have (and as many voters did). Instead of considering it a statement of principles to guide their legislative efforts, a large number of the newly elected House members (and some of the leadership of both houses of Congress) decided that their election was a mandate for intransigence. "Compromise" and "deliberation" became dirty words.

Compromise is a morally neutral term. It can certainly be code for capitulation. (Just refer to President Clinton's position on gays in the military for a crash course in how to execute a 180-degree turn.) On the other hand, failure to compromise can signal immaturity and rigidity. At its best, the ability to compromise is the ability to find common ground, areas of agreement that advance everyone's legitimate interests. If a compromise requires the sacrifice of a core principle, it is merely another word for defeat. On the other hand, if the goal remains unchanged, but we agree to changes in the process for achieving the goal, it is genuine compromise. If we have given way on a critical issue, that is defeat; if we concede a peripheral one, that is compromise. People of good will can disagree about whether a given issue is critical or peripheral, or whether a proposed change in process threatens the goal itself. But people of intelligence and good will understand that a flat refusal to compromise at all is an admission of impotence and vanity.

Perhaps we have always elected people who are more interested in posturing than in legislating. I am willing to believe that we have not invented meanspiritedness and political pandering just in the last few years. Partisan passions ebb and flow. We may even have elected dumber people than some of those I see nightly on the news. But they weren't as visible before the advent of the electronic media. Respect for our political institutions is at an all-time low, or so the helpful polls tell us; but the real culprits can be seen in any mirror. *We* are the ones electing these people; *we* are the ones demanding instant gratification and easy-to-understand simplifications. *We* are the ones who are looking for someone to blame—liberals or the radical right, welfare mothers or corporate interests, Democrats or Republicans. In the last analysis, Pogo was right: I have met the enemy and he is us.*

That's why I try to avoid the legislature. Those people *are* representative.

NOTE

1. Quoted in David O'Brien, *Constitutional Law and Politics,* 2d ed., Vol. 2 (New York: W. W. Norton & Co., 1995).

---

*Pogo was a popular and widely syndicated cartoon series drawn by Walt Kelly that used animal characters to satirize the human condition.

9

The Gay Nineties
and Family Values

★★

My husband and I have five children—my three sons from a prior marriage and his two daughters. They have different talents, interests and personalities. One of them—my middle son—is gay.

I was an advocate of equal rights for gays and lesbians long before any of my own children *had* sexual orientations. This position seems unremarkable to me: I cannot imagine why a society would grant or withhold civil rights based upon someone's sex life. I have generally subscribed to the philosophy of one Mrs. Patrick Campbell, who is alleged to have said, "It doesn't matter what you do in the bedroom as long as you don't do it in the street and frighten the horses."

It has become abundantly clear to me that this is not a widely held attitude. Even people who are kind and tolerant in other arenas seem to have great difficulty with the fact that I *don't* have great difficulty accepting my son or advocating equal rights for gay men

100

and lesbian women. I have had disappointing conversations with friends who are otherwise supportive of civil liberties—conversations in which they suggest that the "gay issue" is an impediment to wider acceptance of the ACLU. This is not a partisan issue; despite the higher tolerance for homophobic rhetoric among fringe Republicans, my experience confirms that this is a thoroughly bipartisan bigotry.

Having said that, honesty also compels me to acknowledge that it has largely been the Republican party that has attempted to use antigay bias to gain political advantage. (This is ironic, since until recently, most political polls have suggested that the majority of gays are Republicans.) With this issue, as with other issues of individual autonomy, the Republican party is divided between traditional Republicans and the radical right. Traditional Republican advocates of limited government generally take the view that personal moral decisions are not the province of the state unless those decisions harm the person or property of someone else. As Barry Goldwater said about gays in the military, we believe "You don't have to *be* straight, you just have to *shoot* straight." If you can do the job at hand, government really has no business prying into your bedroom habits. The right wing of the party, on the other hand, believes that government has a duty to impose "morality" and to stigmatize those who do not conform. They also believe that they should be the ones to define what is morally acceptable.

As a Republican who believes in limited government, I am firmly of the opinion that what two consenting adults do in the privacy of their own bedroom is no business of the state. As a civil libertarian, I am perfectly willing to accommodate people who hate homosexuals; so long as we are dealing with ideology and not with physical or economic harm, their opinions are constitutionally protected. But as the Supreme Court recently affirmed in *Evans* v. *Romer,* the fact that some people don't like them is insufficient reason to place gays at a legal disadvantage. As I told a local antigay "activist" the other day: If you don't like gay people, don't invite them to dinner. But don't tell me that the *government* has to have one set of rules for gay people and one for everybody else, which was essentially the thrust of Colorado's infamous Amendment Two.*

Protecting the rights of bigots to be hateful doesn't always play well in the gay community, just as defending the rights of homosexuals to equality before the law doesn't earn points in some of our area churches. Not too long ago, the town of Richmond, Indiana, was considering an amendment to its human rights ordinance. The amendment would have added the words "sexual orientation" to the other categories in the ordinance; that is, it would have made discrimination against gays in employment, housing, or public accommodations a violation. The Richmond Human Rights Commission held two hearings before deadlocking (and thus defeating the measure). I attended both.

At each hearing, the assembly room was filled to overflowing, with people jamming the halls and outer corridors. Buses in the parking lot attested to the efficiency of a number of churches in transporting their partisans.

---

*Amendment Two changed the Colorado Constitution to invalidate local ordinances extending civil rights to gays and lesbians. But it went even further, requiring another constitutional amendment in order to enact such laws in the future. In essence, it created two separate and decidedly unequal political processes: one for gays and lesbians, and one for everybody else. The Supreme Court struck it down over a chillingly homophobic dissent by Justice Antonin Scalia.

While several opponents of the measure made an effort to be courteous and to couch their objections in terms of public policy, many more demanded that the Human Rights Commission—an arm of civil government—legislate "Christian morality." When still other ministers supported the antidiscrimination measure, they were greeted with catcalls and shouts impugning their credentials as Christians (and in a couple of cases, their manhood).

A few days after the first hearing, at which the vote had been postponed, I received an anguished telephone call from one of the gay students at the local college, who had been working for passage of the ordinance. The Richmond newspaper had been carrying a paid advertisement from one of the churches, and it was vile. "I know we believe in free speech," he told me. "But this ad is so horrible. And it's full of lies. Can't we make the paper stop carrying it?" Evidently, the church was well funded; the full-page ad had run three times.

He faxed me the text, and it certainly lived up to its billing. One of the nicer sentiments expressed was that all gays should die of AIDS, which clearly is a judgment from God. It labeled homosexuals as child molesters and perverts and attacked the idea of tolerance, asserting that the Bible requires godly people to be intolerant of sin and deviance. My student contact was appalled when I told him I intended to congratulate the local newspaper for carrying it, but that is precisely what I did. I began my letter by acknowledging the dilemma the paper must have faced when the ad came in, and how tempting it must have been to reject it. But publication had truly been in the interests of the community. Many people who had not previously understood the need for an antidiscrimination measure were able to see the sick, irrational hate that motivates people to actively harm gays and lesbians. By printing the ravings in the ad, the paper had demonstrated the nature of the problem more graphically than any editorial writer could have.

The paper printed my letter. The ad never ran again. Free speech works.

What *are* "gay rights"? And why is everyone so excited about them? Contrary to the rhetoric emanating from political and religious extremists, gay rights are not "special rights." (Although, as a lesbian friend of mine said wistfully, "Well, they're special to me. I don't have them.") What is meant by "gay rights" is *equality before the law*. Americans are entitled to be treated as individuals, not as members of a group. If I rob a bank, I have committed the offense of robbery. There is no separate offense of robbery by a white person or robbery by a female person. When I go to court (assuming I'm caught—but that is a different chapter), I am entitled to be treated as an individual who broke a law. My punishment should be the same whether I am white, black, gay, straight, Methodist, or Wiccan. Granted, there is an immense difference between this ideal and current reality; nevertheless, for most of us, that is the goal.

If group identity is to be irrelevant before the law, how can we justify treating people badly based not upon their public behavior, but upon their presumed private actions? Despite the efforts of those whose ideal of America is mayonnaise on white bread—a vast, white, Christian, heterosexual, homogenous mass of people who do not divorce, abort, read dirty books, or love inappropriate people—this is and will remain an incredibly diverse country. We don't all have to like each other, but we do have to learn to get along. And that means that people I don't approve of will have the same *legal rights* that I have.

One of the reasons that the "special rights" argument has influenced otherwise reasonable folks is that very few people understand the difference between civil liberties and civil rights—not to mention affirmative action, which is neither.

Civil liberties—as anyone who has read this far knows—are the rights secured to citizens against government infringement. When the argument is made that gays already have the right to equal treatment under the law by virtue of the Fourteenth Amendment, that is (almost) true, *if* we are talking about civil liberties. (I say almost, because the courts haven't always caught on. But I certainly agree that the Fourteenth Amendment *ought* to be sufficient to protect gays and lesbians from government shenanigans.)

Civil rights, on the other hand, entitle us to freedom from discrimination by nongovernmental employers, landlords, and proprietors of public accommodations. Civil liberties don't do a whole lot of good if the only factory in town can decide not to hire women, the only apartment complex won't rent to African-Americans, and the diner won't serve Jews. Civil rights statutes prohibit such private sector discrimination. While the ACLU is a civil liberties organization, we favor civil rights laws. So, historically, has the Republican party. Both would agree that there must be limits to government's authority to require equal treatment by private parties. Unlike restraints on government action, civil rights laws restrict the freedom of those who are discriminating and thus must be carefully crafted and narrowly targeted. Religious enterprises must be allowed to insist on conformity with doctrine, for example, even if that doctrine operates in a discriminatory manner. The behavior of private parties not engaged in commerce cannot be compelled. But within the limits imposed, we agree with most Americans that

businesses ought not be able to reject people for characteristics having nothing to do with their performance
as employees or their behavior as tenants or customers. Currently, in 1997, gays are protected against
such discrimination in exactly nine states (and some
assorted cities).

My city and state are not among those that include
sexual orientation under our civil rights laws, so when
someone calls our help line to report that he has been
fired because his boss found out he is gay, and doesn't
want any "damn faggot" working for him, I have to say,
"Too bad. There is absolutely nothing you can do about
it. It doesn't matter that you've worked there ten years
and never had a complaint. You have no rights that the
law will recognize." Civil rights statutes generally forbid
private employers or landlords to discriminate on the
basis of race, national origin, religion, gender, or disability. But in most states, if you want to fire someone
for being gay, go right ahead. If an apartment complex
wants to exclude gays, no problem. It is protection from
these kinds of discrimination, the same protection en-
joyed by the other enumerated minorities, that is the
focus of efforts by the gay community. "Gay rights"
means freedom from being picked on and disadvantaged for no reason other than one's sexual orientation.

The elements most vocal in opposition to civil rights
for gays and lesbians don't talk about nondiscrimination; they talk in terms of affirmative action, and what
they mean by affirmative action is government-re-
quired proportional hiring programs. It doesn't take the
proverbial rocket scientist to see the fallacy in such
suggestions. Unlike women and blacks, gays are not
readily identifiable for purposes of constructing utilization tables. Many (perhaps most) are still in the closet.
And most would be eternally grateful just to have some

legal recourse when they are subjected to blatant discrimination. This argument is a cynical play on homophobia and the public's general discomfort with affirmative action programs.

In the last three years, I have probably heard every argument ever made against extending civil rights to the gay community. Most are based upon religious doctrine. Members of churches teaching that homosexuality is evil are, of course, entitled to that belief. They are even entitled to proclaim that belief in the "public square" and the ACLU will protect their right to do so. But they are not entitled to have civil authority legislate on the basis of their religious beliefs. If homosexuality is truly against God's law, I'm confident God will be able to deal with the transgressors without the assistance of the United States government or its political subdivisions.

Other justifications are offered for continuing to discriminate against gay men and lesbian women:

"We must protect children." Then lock up all the heterosexuals, because all available data confirms that heterosexuals constitute the *vast* majority of child molesters. This argument is the clearest example of demonizing—and people who make it are themselves the best evidence of the existence of irrational antigay bias. Of course, all groups, including homosexuals, have their bad apples. As I told one earnest fellow, "Pedophilia is terrible—I agree that we should do everything we can to protect children. But just because so many incidents of molestation occur in churches is no reason to discriminate against all the good religious people."

"We cannot endorse deviant behavior." Leaving aside the definition of what constitutes "deviant behavior," we are not talking about erecting statues in the public parks. We are talking about government's obligation to ensure equal *legal* status for all citizens. There are plenty of people of whom I do not approve, but my disapproval is not grounds for denying them civil rights. This is the same flawed logic that says if I support your right to free speech, I must agree with everything you say. Many religions teach that divorce is a sin; shall we deny divorced individuals their civil rights?

"Being gay is a behavior, not an identity. People choose to be gay; they don't choose to be black or female." People choose to be Presbyterian, too—but we have laws against discrimination based upon religion. (Actually, the evidence is fairly clear that homosexuality is at least partly genetic. It is interesting how many of the people who insist that being gay is a "lifestyle choice" that can be turned on and off with just a little willpower are the same ones who brag to friends that they can "always spot one.") More to the point, prejudice and discrimination against people who are gay *or* who are perceived to be gay is undeniable. Civil rights protection is appropriate when people are singled out for unequal treatment based solely upon their membership in a particular group. If there is any doubt that homophobia is not based upon behavior, think about the harassment suffered by high school youngsters who have yet to have any sort of sexual encounter—homosexual or heterosexual. People who bully gays do not require evidence of actual sexual activity to trigger their animosities; characteristics which they (rightly or wrongly) attribute to homosexuals are sufficient.

"If we make sexual orientation a protected class, who's next? Fat people? Cross-eyed people? Isn't this just more identity politics?" I have some sympathy for this argument. While diversity can be a great strength, too much insistence on our differences can erode the sense of community that makes us first and foremost Americans. We have an obligation to document the need for antidiscrimination measures—just as we should document the need for *any* government action. Inclusion as a suspect class for purposes of civil rights protection should be based upon a finding that systemic, long-term discrimination exists, and that it operates to disadvantage people as a class. If anyone doubts that sexual orientation meets that criterion, just "hang out" on the ICLU Intake line for a few days, or answer the telephone for Justice, Inc., a gay civil-rights group. Their answering machine routinely records messages like "All you faggots are going to burn in hell," and "You'd better watch where you drive and walk, you queers, because I'm going to kill you and all of your perverted kind."

"The number of gays has been grossly exaggerated." This one mystifies me. Why do numbers matter? Are definable groups entitled to basic civil rights only if they exceed some magic threshold percentage of the population? To ask the question is (one hopes!) to answer it. Gay men and lesbians are entitled to basic civil liberties whether they number fifty or fifty million. It is doubtful that we can estimate the gay population accurately, in any event; how many homosexual encounters qualify one as "gay"? How many frightened gays refuse to admit their orientation to *themselves,* let alone to a poll taker? Respected national pollsters like Lou Harris will be the first to acknowledge the inadequacy of polling instruments for measuring sexual identity. According to Harris, and most political pollsters, poll results are inherently unreliable in three areas: drug use, religious observance, and sexual behavior.

"Legislation should promote 'family values.'" I agree

wholeheartedly. But being "for" family values does not require one to be "against" civil rights for gay men and lesbian women, any more than it requires discriminating against women who work outside the home, or against single-parent families. There is certainly ample evidence of the desirability of raising children in intact, monogamous homes. To put it another way, all things being equal, it is preferable for children to be raised in emotionally healthy, socially supported family units. There is also lots of evidence to indicate that children raised in financially secure families do better emotionally and intellectually—but I hope that few of us would suggest depriving the poor of their basic civil rights or their right to parent their children. The well-being of children is generally what people are talking about when they raise "family values" as an issue; however, increasing numbers of families do not include children. For those families, child-centered concerns are irrelevant.

If the question is how we shall support all families without inadvertently undermining the family types which we deem most beneficial, the issue is entirely legitimate and deserving of our careful attention. If, however, we decide that since the majority has deemed family type A preferable, we will punish and marginalize family type B, that is a different matter entirely. Government has an obligation to treat citizens equally, without favoritism or bias. Agreement with the principal of government even-handedness is not contrary to "family values." It is a necessary condition to the creation of a society that values families.

Of course, if we were really interested in promoting committed, stable, long-term relationships, we would allow gay couples to publicly affirm their unions. According to U.S. Census statistics, heterosexual couples, who enjoy broad social support for our marriages, have nearly a 50 percent failure rate. And we have the nerve to be judgmental when gay couplings—subject to inconceivable stress and no official sanction or support—don't last?

The issue is equity. For decades, the military has been a primary vehicle for social mobility and education for people who otherwise could not afford either. All Americans support the military with our taxes, and all of us—subject to physical and mental ability to do the job—may join. Except gays. (And it won't do to argue that being gay is by definition an inability to do the job. No fewer than five studies commissioned by the Pentagon itself have concluded that the only impediment to service by those who are openly gay is the bigotry of heterosexual servicemen.[1]) Our tax system rewards those of us who marry with favorable rates, while taxpayers in even the most long-term gay relationships pay more. Health insurance benefits are usually available to spouses and children; few companies allow gay employees to cover their partners. Without legal documentation, gay partners cannot visit each other in restricted hospital areas, inherit from each other if one partner dies intestate, or benefit from a panoply of institutions that heterosexual marrieds take for granted. Even if gays were not subject to overt bias, such disadvantages are patently unfair.

The bottom line is that it is never just to categorize or stereotype people on the basis of a single characteristic. As the workforce has become more integrated, blacks and whites have begun to shed stereotypes about race; interreligious organizations have helped us see beyond religious typecasting. Unfortunately, because gays look like everyone else, because they live in all kinds of families, and because until very recently they have usually not identified themselves, the only image many people have of gay men is that of the drag queen; the only image of lesbian women, that of "dykes on bikes." Just as all Jews are not Hasidim, all gays are not represented by such individuals. But until many, many more gays "come out" there will not be an accurate understanding of the immense diversity within the gay community.

I was engaged in a real estate transaction not long ago with a local businessman. We talked a bit about the ICLU, and the issue of "gay rights" came up. He was genuinely curious when he asked me what I thought the gay community wanted. When I told him that my gay friends simply wanted to be able to live ordinary lives—to acknowledge (*not* flaunt, just acknowledge) their relationships or identities without fear of losing a job or being evicted from housing or being beaten up—he persisted. Why, if there was no larger agenda, was he seeing so many newspaper articles about people "coming out"? What purpose does it serve to "advertise" if all one wants is to be allowed to live in peace? I told him about a PFlag meeting held on October 11. PFlag is an acronym for Parents, Families and Friends of Lesbians and Gays. October 11 is national "Coming Out Day"—a day devoted to encouraging gays and lesbians to come out of the closet and publicly affirm their identities.

Why? Why should gays abandon the comparative safety of the closet? Why should we, their families, come out to friends and relatives? After all, those of us who are heterosexual rarely find it necessary to trumpet that fact, or to tell our neighbors that our children are heterosexual. Isn't it kind of tacky to talk about our sex lives anyway?

If gays and lesbians were not subjected to hatred and discrimination, there would be no reason to come out, but in a world where they are routinely demonized, it is immensely important. People who think they don't know anyone gay (are you listening, Senator Helms?) need to be confronted with the reality that they know many. They just don't *know* they know them. Such people also need to meet families—parents, grandparents, and siblings—who love and accept our children *as they are.*

I can accept my son—easily. What I cannot and will not accept is a society that treats him differently than it treats his brothers, for no other reason than the gender of those he loves. That—not his sexual orientation—is what is unacceptable. That—not his orientation—is what is immoral.

If we don't all come out, parents as well as gay men and lesbians, we are feeding the homophobia and enabling the demonization. It is so much easier to refer to "those perverts" when we don't know any as human beings. When we discover that "those perverts" include sweet Aunt Gladys, or Cousin Jerry's middle boy who used to mow our lawn, or the mailman, or our doctor, or our business partner—it becomes much more difficult to divide the world into "us" and "them."

Are there awful gay people? Promiscuous gay people? Of course. Just as there are awful Jews, promiscuous Baptists, dishonest Hispanics . . . the list is as endless as humanity. Every group has good people and bad. By coming out, gays and their families force others to confront human beings rather than cartoons. By coming out, we insist upon identity, not anonymity. We serve as a reminder that no single characteristic defines a human being—not race, not religion, not sexual orientation. People are entitled to be treated as individuals. By coming out, gays and their families force others to respond to us on that basis.

Contemporary political rhetoric is rife with references to "family values." I have rarely seen better examples of family values than at PFlag meetings, where parents who love and accept their children have undertaken to improve the society in which those children must live. PFlag brings together people who have absolutely nothing in common except love for their children and rejection of hate and homophobia. For some, it has been a difficult and hurtful journey; for others, as natural as breathing. What we share is a very primal emotion—a fierce devotion to our children and a resolve not to let ignorance and intolerance hurt them. A bumper sticker popular with PFlag parents sums it up: Hate is not a family value.

In 1994, PFlag gave its national Flag Bearer's Award to Barry Goldwater. The Flag Bearer's award is given annually to prominent people who have spoken out against discrimination. In addition to Goldwater, Republican Governor William Weld of Massachusetts has recently been honored by PFlag for his efforts to make the public schools safer for gay youth. If the willingness of such Republicans to speak out seems surprising, it shouldn't. At the grassroots level, the Republican party has largely resisted the temptation to adopt homophobic positions. Log Cabin Republicans, who support gay rights, have proliferated. In the last election in my congressional district, both the Republican and Democratic candidates actively solicited the gay vote. Where local governments have enacted antidiscrimination ordinances, Republicans as well as Democrats have supported those laws.

You either believe that government belongs in your bedroom or you don't. Most Republicans, like most members of the ACLU, don't.

NOTE

1. See Kate Dyer, ed., *Gays in the Military: The Pentagon's Secret Reports* (Boston: Alyson, 1990).

10

The "Criminal's Lobby" versus Tax and Spend Conservatives

★★★

If there is any issue that would seem to separate law and order Republicans from civil libertarians, crime and punishment would surely be it. Or would it?

On the jacket of his recent book, *Ain't Nobody's Business if You Do,*[1] Peter McWilliams sums up what is wrong with America's criminal justice system. "Solving the problems [of crime]" he says, "is going to take commitment, creativity, money, and a lot of work—precisely the resources currently squandered in the futile attempt to regulate individual morality." McWilliams's book is a readable and very sane argument for limiting our definition of crimes to actions that physically harm the person or property of another. In laudable capitalist fashion, he points out that the elimination of victimless crimes (which he calls "consensual crimes") would wipe out the national debt in twenty years; instead, current policies will *add* a trillion—yes, *trillion*—dollars to that debt in the space of only five years.

116

I know of no one in the ACLU who would argue with the proposition that it is government's duty to keep order and provide for the public safety. This is a basic and legitimate function of the state. It requires that the state prohibit certain activities—*criminalize* them—and that it punish those who do not comply, removing them from society if they pose a danger to others. My guess is that Republicans and civil libertarians will also agree that crimes should be narrowly and precisely defined; and that the ideal criminal justice system should be effective, just, and cost-effective.

There are many reasons we should insist upon precise descriptions of those actions which society deems criminal. The most obvious is that citizens have a right to know, without ambiguity, what is prohibited and what is not. (Ask any businessman who finds himself drowning in a sea of impenetrable regulations, violation of which carry hefty penalties, how fair it is that he must hire a lawyer to figure out what he is allowed to do. Then ask yourself how that situation differs from most laws proscribing obscenity. Even a Supreme Court justice was reduced to admitting he couldn't define obscene material, falling back on "I know it when I see it." I'm sure *that* gave bookstores and movie producers ample direction!) Clarity of the law is a basic requirement of justice.

The importance of narrow definition is less well understood. By "narrow" I mean limiting those actions that are considered criminal to the minimum required to achieve public safety. In a free country, we necessarily depend upon voluntary compliance with the law—and despite what we see on the television evening news and in the tabloids, most people *do* voluntarily comply. We also depend upon the vast majority of law-abiding citizens to create an environment that supports the rule of law and encourages compliance. Any police officer will confirm that peer pressure, where available, is the most effective ally of law enforcement. In order to create this "culture of compliance," however, our criminal laws must be viewed as appropriate. When legislators criminalize behaviors that most people consider harmless, behaviors that large numbers of people engage in, the moral authority of the law disappears. When everything from murder to underage tobacco purchase is a crime, crime becomes no big deal. When laws are enacted with full knowledge that they cannot and will not be enforced (sodomy and seat belt laws come to mind, but there are many others) in order to "send a message," the message *really* sent is—in Charles Dickens's felicitous phrase—"the law is a ass."

It would be bad enough if people simply lost respect for the laws that are silly or excessive, but what happens is much worse: When large numbers of people can "thumb their nose" at some laws, it breeds disrespect for *all* legal authority. We saw the effect of Prohibition on law enforcement generally; it was a disaster. When the law proposes to regulate too many behaviors, it loses the ability to regulate any of them very effectively. But the damage of overreaching doesn't stop there. When we give government extra power, there is extra potential for abuse. When we make laws regulating sexual behavior between consenting adults, we turn police officers into peeping toms; when we forbid people to smoke pot, we encourage petty extortion; when we criminalize behaviors that do not harm the person or property of others, we trivialize the rule of law itself.

If our common goal is a criminal justice system that is effective, just, and cost-effective, how do we define those terms? May I suggest that we start with the hy-

pothesis that in an *effective* system, we will be *safer*? If
that seems elementary, it certainly hasn't occurred to
most of the folks who are proposing and enacting our
criminal laws. (Can we imagine a doctor performing
hundreds of operations without curing anyone saying,
"Well, we just need to do a lot *more* of that!" How long
would he be practicing medicine?) But "Does this
work?" would appear to be the *last* thing our lawmakers consider. An effective system would, at a minimum, catch and punish most wrongdoers (certainty of
even relatively light punishment has been shown to be
more of a deterrent than significant penalties that are
statistically unlikely to be imposed.[2]) And an effective
system would rehabilitate criminals before returning
them to society. (I am willing to concede this one, for
the simple reason that we don't seem to have a clue
how to rehabilitate people, but we ought to keep trying.
If we ever figure it out, it will save us immense human
and financial problems.)

Of course, we could have a system that meets my
criteria for effectiveness that Americans would not tol-
erate. Singapore comes to mind. Despite all the macho
talk at cocktail parties and on talk radio in 1994 when
American teenager Michael Fay was caned for van-
dalism (he spraypainted a row of cars), a system like
that would last about fifteen minutes with our cranky,
independent, and fundamentally fair-minded citizenry.
So in addition to being effective, the criminal justice
system must live up to its name—it must be a system
that metes out justice.

A *just* system will treat everyone alike—rich, poor,
black, white, whatever. It will ensure fair proceedings
to determine innocence or guilt, avoiding undue advantage to the state with its superior power and resources. This was a major concern of the founders and

a prime motivation for the Fourth, Fifth, and Sixth Amendments.* The goal of a criminal trial should be to determine truth insofar as possible. It is amazing how many people seem more interested in vengeance than in finding out whether the accused is the proper target for that vengeance. A just system will also apply penalties that are proportional to the transgression—the punishment will fit the crime. (This, admittedly, can be pretty subjective.) And in a just system, there will be an emphasis upon restitution, upon making the victim whole, if possible.

A *cost-effective system* is one that keeps law-abiding citizens safe both from criminals and the criminal justice system itself while spending the fewest possible tax dollars. If I may use a term rarely employed in this context, it will be *efficient.*

Now, if the ACLU and most Republicans agree on most of those goals, why do even mainstream Republicans consider the ACLU "liberal" or "soft" on crime? Why is the organization sneeringly referred to by self-styled law and order types as "the criminal's lobby"?

The so-called War on Drugs may be the issue that most divides the ACLU from politicians of both parties. Public rhetoric being what it is, opposition to drug laws is seen as condoning or even promoting drug use. That is an illogical conclusion. It is a result of asking the wrong questions. If the question is, are drugs bad, the answer is yes. (I realize that many people will argue that certain drugs aren't harmful, but most of us agree

---

*The Fourth Amendment provides protection against unreasonable search and seizure; the Fifth provides for due process as well as protects against double jeopardy (being tried twice for the same crime) and compelling one to testify against himself; and the Sixth provides for a speedy trial, the right to confront witnesses, and the right to counsel.

that the recreational use of drugs is something society ought to discourage.) The trouble is, that *isn't* the question. The question is, should every misuse of such substances be criminalized? Assuming that we actually want to reduce the incidence of drug use, does criminalization work? Is it moving us closer to that goal? And what are the costs involved? But no one wants even to discuss these questions. It has become politically incorrect to question current drug policies.

Recently, I had a call from a high school teacher who was trying to arrange a debate on the pros and cons of the drug war. He was frustrated, because he had spoken privately to a number of judges, police officers, and prosecutors in his community, and—off the record—every one of them had expressed the opinion that in its current form, the drug war is doing more harm than good. Yet when he asked them to share their reservations in a public forum, every one of them declined. They feared being labeled soft on crime. There is nothing wrong with being conflicted over the best way to approach America's drug problem. There is something very wrong when we can't even look at a program to see if it works or discuss how it might be made more effective.

Federal, state, and local spending on drug control has grown 760 percent since 1981. Sixty-seven government agencies (not counting state and local entities) are listed in the National Drug Control budget. This country has spent over a *hundred billion dollars* since 1980, according to official estimates (and a whole lot more, according to unofficial ones) to eradicate drugs and drug use. And this does *not* include the taxes we could have imposed on these transactions—money that could have been used for drug education and treatment. Education has been extremely effective in reducing use of tobacco—

a substance more addictive than many of the substances we prohibit. There is no reason to believe that it could not be equally effective with other drugs.

During the last fifteen years of constantly escalating spending, prosecuting, and imprisoning, have things gotten better? Virtually all agencies reporting on the war on drugs agree that it has failed on every front. Drugs are still readily available. The price of street drugs has risen, along with the criminal activity of addicts seeking money to buy those drugs and the earnings of drug dealers who become ever more violent protecting their ever-more-profitable turf. (Profits are courtesy of the laws prohibiting legal sale. The market really does work.) Over 60 percent of the people incarcerated in federal prisons are there for drug-related offenses. Mandatory minimum drug sentencing has replaced the discretion of the judge with that of the government prosecutor. Those mandatory minimums have also forced the release of many violent offenders who weren't sentenced under such mandates, in order to make room for nonviolent drug offenders.

Peter McWilliams points out that the war on drugs is often defended by those who want to protect children, but that it is the children who are most endangered when we criminalize rather than regulate. Liquor stores generally are vigilant in their efforts not to sell to minors; as a regulated, but legal, enterprise, they don't need or want the hassle. However, the artificially high prices for drugs created by criminalization make finding new customers—like those in schoolyards—tempting. Dealers are already outside the law; they have nothing to lose and much to gain by preying on easy underage targets. Regulation would also insure "quality control," making it less likely that drugs have been cut with lethal substances.

There are innumerable other problems with the nation's drug war: Some constitutional scholars have suggested that we haven't become drug free, just *less* free. In the name of drug interdiction, we have trampled on the civil liberties of innocent people. So-called civil forfeiture laws have robbed innocent spouses of life savings; mandatory drug testing of people not suspected of drug use has invaded the privacy of ordinary citizens; wiretapping has been used indiscriminately. And in return for relinquishing these freedoms, what have we achieved?

Has the war on drugs made us safer? Has it increased the esteem in which we hold the justice system? Has it treated all offenders equally? Have most offenders been caught? Do the punishments meted out fit the crimes committed? Has the war on drugs been cost-effective? If the answer to all of these questions is no—and it is—*why aren't we talking about alternative approaches?*

If looking at the facts makes the ACLU "liberal," so be it. If pointing out that the emperor has no clothes, that the war on drugs is not working, makes us "soft on crime," the term has no meaning. It was Milton Friedman, the noted Republican economist, who said, "I'm in favor of legalizing drugs. According to my value system, if people want to kill themselves, they have every right to do so. Most of the harm that comes from drugs is because they are illegal."[3] I'm not sure that I would go as far as Friedman, although a full public debate on the issue might convince me. Many in the ACLU do agree with Milton Friedman, William F. Buckley Jr., and other well-known "liberals" on the drug issue. But while I may or may not agree with Friedman, I am absolutely sure I agree with Elizabeth Cady Stanton, who said, "To make laws that man cannot and will not obey serves to bring all law into contempt."

If the ACLU position on the drug war raises suspicion about our commitment to law and order, our opposition to the death penalty confirms that we are simply a group of leftover flower children from the 1960s, soft-hearted muddle heads who care more about the criminal than the victim. At least it isn't Republicans who level those charges. It's *everyone*. The death penalty is more popular than Elvis ever was. As reports of violent crime escalate (and the *reports* certainly have; FBI statistics indicate that violent crime itself has actually fallen off of late), citizens rise up in righteous wrath and demand that we "fry them."

Well, why not? I will confess that I am not among those who believe the state is never morally justified in taking a life. I think that commission of certain crimes can be said to merit the ultimate punishment. But I also believe that giving government the power to kill imposes enormous responsibilities on those administering the system—responsibilities we are not discharging and probably cannot discharge. And—forgive my crass, capitalistic nature—the death penalty is just too expensive.

Let's take a quick look at the justifications for execution of wrongdoers. The most common is deterrence. And it is certainly true that capital punishment deters those we kill. But it is equally clear that the death penalty doesn't deter anyone else. Even ardent proponents admit as much. Since 1982, Texas has executed at least ninety-two people, more than any other state. In 1991, Texas had the third highest crime rate in the United States, and the *second* highest murder rate. (That's *rate*, not number.) Most murders are crimes of passion; they are not committed by people coolly weighing the likelihood of capture, conviction, and execution. New York Assistant District Attorney Robert Morgenthau (a Republican, by the way—but of course he's from New York so it probably doesn't count) has pointed out that the number of homicides in Manhattan was cut in half, without the help of a death penalty.

There is also the inconvenient fact that we keep executing people who are innocent. It is awfully hard to make amends for that sort of mistake. A study published in the *Stanford Law Review* has documented 350 capital convictions in this century in which it was later proven that the person convicted had not committed the crime.[4] Twenty-five of those people were executed, twenty of them between 1980 and 1985. I recently debated a law school professor who is a zealous defender of the death penalty. His response to the Stanford statistics was, well, mistakes happen. When we inoculate children against smallpox, there is a risk some will die of the vaccination. A margin of error is something he is prepared to accept, even though human lives are involved. I wonder if he would be quite so sanguine if *he* were the one mistakenly on death row. More to the point, if we are trying to create a society in which the crime of murder is unthinkable, a casual attitude toward mistaken executions doesn't exactly convey the idea that human life is sacred.

And while we are on the subject of inconvenient facts, let's talk about the O. J. Simpson and Susan Smith trials. (I know—I'm sick of them too, but there is a point to be made here.) Both were accused of truly horrible crimes. Simpson was accused of brutally murdering his ex-wife Nicole and her friend Ron Goldman in California in June 1994; the same year, Susan Smith was tried for driving her car into a South Carolina lake and intentionally drowning her two young sons. The prosecution sought the death penalty against Susan Smith. It did not seek that penalty against O. J. Simpson. One could argue that this disparity merely reflects the essentially local nature of law enforcement, which naturally will lead to inconsistencies. If one accepts that argument, imposition of the death penalty depends upon where you commit your crime—a fairly arbitrary factor in itself. The truth of the matter, however, is that the difference cannot reasonably be attributed to anything but money. O. J. had enough to hire private counsel; Susan Smith did not. Those high-profile prosecutions simply showed the general public what lawyers have known for years: the only people we put to death are poor people. Prosecutors rarely ask for the death penalty in cases where the accused has private legal counsel rather than an overworked public defender. When they do, criminals with money for adequate representation can virtually always plea-bargain. And there is another nasty little statistic: The vast majority of people on death row were convicted of killing a white person. The race of the perpetrator is not dispositive, but the race of the *victim* frequently is. I do not suggest that this is intentional; it simply reflects the reality that Americas still place a higher value on white lives than on black ones.

One could argue that killing people to demonstrate that we are a society that doesn't believe in killing people is, shall we say, counterintuitive. But being a fiscal conservative, I find the cost argument to be the most compelling. Most people seem to believe that keeping a criminal incarcerated for the rest of his or her life is more expensive than execution. Wrong—very wrong. We pay enormous sums to kill people, by some estimates as much as seven times what it would cost to warehouse the convict until natural death. In Indiana, according to a government study, the average cost to a county of trying a capital case is $138,000; the cost of trying a noncapital case is $25,000. That does not include appeals, post-conviction petitions, etc. It also does not include any of the costs of incarceration. And Indiana's costs are comparatively low. In 1992, a study by the Dallas *Morning News* found that death penalty cases each cost Texas taxpayers $2,300,000. (That *did* include appeals.) Florida calculated the total cost of each execution—trial, appeals, incarceration pending execution, etc.—at $3,200,000.[5]

Of course, a substantial portion of this expense is due to the appeals process. Proponents of "swift and certain justice" argue that we should drastically curtail appeals. Most advocates of this solution are not sitting on death row, innocent of a crime they were convicted of in a trial featuring an inadequate defense by an overwhelmed public defender. If at least twenty-five innocent people have been executed during the last decade by a system that allows a full appeal process, how many more innocent people will be killed when appeals are no longer available? Given the gross imbalance between prosecution and defense in most death penalty trials, cutting off appeals would be tantamount to an admission that we don't really care if the accused is guilty or just unlucky. Frustrating and duplicative as the appellate process can be, I think that most Americans who support the death penalty do want to be sure we are killing the right person.

Is the death penalty effective? As vengeance, probably; as a deterrent to others, not at all. Does it apply equally to everyone who has committed the same type of crime? Is our margin of error as low as possible? Is it cost-effective? If the answer to all these questions is no, hasn't it become "cruel and unusual" for purposes of the Eighth Amendment? And can't we find a less expensive method for exacting social retribution? I am all in favor of locking convicted murderers away for life, without parole. That way, they can't hurt anyone else, and if it turns out they are innocent, they can go home.

★　★　★

Aside from hot-button issues like the drug war and capital punishment, the ACLU gets jaundiced looks whenever we call police to task for inappropriate behaviors. We are seen as making it harder for public safety officials whose jobs are already difficult. But is that really what we are doing?

One of the painful lessons I learned from parenting was that telling my children "Do as I say, not as I do" didn't work. We can all moralize about telling the truth, but if our children see us lie, they conclude that lying is really okay. If mom and dad preach that drugs are bad, but regularly get drunk on martinis, it sends a somewhat mixed message. Congress took a lot of justifiable criticism for passing laws from which it exempted itself. After all, if the laws were such great ideas, why didn't Congress follow them too? For some reason, people don't perceive the same issue in the context of police/citizen interaction.

There are two good reasons to insist that government follow its own rules, even when dealing with "bad guys." The first is that failure to do so is counterproductive. It sends a mixed message. Why should a young hoodlum believe in and abide by the rule of law if the officer arresting him doesn't? In that case, the criminal sees the issue strictly as one of power—not the power that is implicit in right behavior and ethical superiority, but the power of the gun. Government loses its moral authority when it ignores the very legal system it purports to enforce.

The second reason to insist that government follow the rules is that the alternative is dangerous. We may applaud when Dirty Harry uses illegal tactics to get the bad guys, but the policeman who can abuse a scumbag with impunity today can abuse law abiding citizens with equal impunity tomorrow.

Does an insistence on following the rules make police work more difficult? Quite probably, and it is recognition of that fact that leads most of us to give officers the benefit of the doubt in close cases. As every parent can confirm, setting a good example is a lot harder than just telling children "Do as I say, not as I do." But in both cases—parenting and policing—it works better. Good police officers understand that. At the ICLU, we often get calls from police who are concerned about the propriety of public safety initiatives. (We are also the first place they call when their *own* civil liberties are violated.) While it would be inaccurate to suggest that the majority of police officers agree with us on all issues, much of the public would be astonished at how extensive the areas of agreement are.

There is a great deal of political posturing involved in these and other crime issues, and the rhetoric makes it difficult to separate fact from fiction. In Indiana, one of the people most knowledgeable about the criminal justice system is a conservative Republican lawyer and former state senator named Leslie Duvall. Retired now, Les served for many years as chair of the Senate Judiciary Committee. He contributed a very thoughtful piece to the ICLU newsletter last year. Entitled "A Conservative Looks at Criminal Justice," the essay contained a number of points worth considering.

Les began by listing basic tenets of his conservatism: fiscal restraint (making sure that tax revenues are spent prudently and in a cost-effective manner); local control in preference to the growing federalism of criminal justice measures; and strict construction (allowing only such government action as is specifically authorized by the Constitution and the Bill of Rights).

According to Les, "The basic purpose of government is to protect the lives and property of its citizens." How do we accomplish this? We begin by punishing offenders. But "punishment is based on different concepts. These are retribution, incapacitation, deterrence, restitution and reformation. . . . Punishment based on retribution or revenge does nothing to enhance public safety. It satisfies to some degree our revulsion of the crime and incorporates some sense of justice based on a 'just desserts' [sic] rationale. It is a natural, emotional reaction to crime, but it does not enhance public safety." After discussing capital punishment ("While it may be justifiable to support capital punishment, it cannot be done on the basis of deterrence. There is simply no evidence to support that theory"); the importance of restitution ("It is only through restitution that the victim and community can be made whole, as well as the offender"); and the need to concentrate on reformation ("Obviously, it is that which will do the most to ensure public safety"); he discussed the monumental costs of our "lock 'em all up" mentality ("Building a maximum security prison costs approximately $80,000 per prison bed. . . . The annual cost per prisoner will run $15,000"). After pointing out that the current frenzy to build more prisons will cost billions of tax dollars and will have a very questionable effect on public safety, he ended his essay with a reminder that the ability of government is finite:

Conservatives should recognize that government can never solve our crime problems. Conservatives, above all, should recognize that at its roots, crime is a moral choice, that the institutions of family and the church will ultimately frame those moral choices. The conservative should be the last to legislate based on slogans such as "three strikes and you're out" and "truth in sentencing." Finally, everyone—conservative and liberal, should ask himself, "What am *I* doing to address the problem of crime in *my* neighborhood?"[6]

I wish some of those tax and spend conservatives in Washington were listening.

NOTES

1. Peter McWilliams, *Ain't Nobody's Business If You Do: The Absurdity of Consensual Crimes in a Free Society* (Los Angeles: Prelude Press, 1993).

2. Cited by Campaign for an Effective Crime Policy, 918 F Street NW, Washington, D.C.

3. Quoted in McWilliams, *Ain't Nobody's Business.*

4. "Discrimination and Arbitrariness in Capital Punishment," *Stanford Law Review* 33 (November 1980): 25–101.

5. Cheri Harris, *Common Ground* 1, no. 1 (1992).

6. Leslie Duvall, "A Conservative Looks at Criminal Justice," *The Advocate* 12, no. 2 (Spring 1994): 14.

11

Disagreeing with National
on Affirmative Action

★★★

There is an old legal maxim to the effect that "He who frames the issue, wins the debate." The answers I get depend upon the questions I ask.

Current political discussions are characterized by an absence of nuance or complexity; instead, questions are generally posed as mutually inconsistent alternatives. Should we continue affirmative action or should we discontinue it? Has affirmative action succeeded or has it failed? Is the United States committed to racial equality or are we witnessing a wholesale retreat into racism? Real life can rarely be reduced to such "either/or" formulations.

While one would have to live on another planet to conclude that we have conquered racism in America, it is possible to disagree about remedies.

Despite the wholesale commitment of the ACLU to affirmative action, I have reluctantly concluded that most of those programs are not only the wrong way to bridge the very real racial divisions in this country, but are contrary to basic civil liberties principles. I think we have been asking the wrong questions.

Rather than framing the issue of affirmative action as a "zero-sum" game, we need to pose a series of different queries: What are our goals? Which efforts move us closer to those goals? Is public hostility to affirmative action just racism wearing a different hat, or does it signal genuine problems with these programs themselves? And what do we mean by affirmative action, anyway?

For a long time, I chose not to voice misgivings about race-based remedies, in part because so many of the attacks on those programs come from sources whose commitment to racial equality is—to be charitable—suspect, and in part because I didn't want to open myself to attack by those who are inclined to view any criticism of affirmative action as part of an "attempt to roll back the rights of America's disenfranchised," as the Michigan ACLU recently charged in a fundraising letter. I certainly didn't want to confirm the suspicion of many in the ACLU that all Republicans are closeted bigots. But there are principled reasons to be concerned about some of the social engineering that is motivated by guilt over our very real social sins.

There are three broad categories of activity encompassed by the term "affirmative action." Depending upon the context of the discussion, affirmative action may mean one or all of them.

The broadest category springs from a sense of moral obligation to members of groups, notably African-Americans, victimized by racial animus. It encompasses various private efforts to heighten sensitivity to cultural differences and to bridge different communication styles. Promotion of multiculturalism and efforts at "political correctness" derive from a recognition that real people have suffered real harm for no reason other than their skin color, that we are a long way from eradicating racism, and that our society has an obligation to address and remedy the harms done.

The second category includes voluntary efforts by institutions and businesses to achieve a broader diversity, to "look like America." These efforts are frequently fueled by an informed self-interest. In an increasingly multiethnic, multiracial society, it is good for business when customers see people like themselves behind the counter or at a presentation. Colleges know that students learn from each other, and that providing a diverse student body is an important component of the educational experience.

The third category is legal mandates. Those come in two varieties: court-imposed remedies for specific, proven acts of discrimination and requirements set by the government as a condition of obtaining a government contract or funding, irrespective of past behavior.

I am convinced that this last effort—mandated inclusion irrespective of prior specific wrongdoing—generates most public hostility to affirmative action. For purposes of this discussion, when I refer to affirmative action, I am talking only about those governmental programs.

At its core, the American system is based upon the notion of individual rights and obligations. Just as we see our entitlements as individual, we see guilt as personal. No matter how often we fall short of our ideal of a race-blind society, it does remain the goal. So long as affirmative action means (as it initially did) taking affirmative steps to ensure individual rights and to punish individual miscreants, I believe most Americans see those measures as appropriate.

There is a fundamental difference between ordering the local widget manufacturer to engage in proportional hiring until he has made amends for deliberate bias, and insisting that an arguably blameless widgeteer justify the racial or sexual composition of his workforce. True, in both cases, the minorities who get hired need not be those who personally suffered from the discriminatory behavior, and the white males who might otherwise have been hired are personally blameless; yet most of us instinctively understand the distinction. If my father cheated yours, and both die, you have a right to recover your rightful inheritance from my father's estate. If you do not, I am unjustly enriched. Your right and my obligation are seen as real, even though you were not the victim and I was not the culprit. When I attempt to stretch this metaphor to create a societal responsibility, however, the causal link snaps. You are being asked to surrender part of your inheritance because my father cheated a third party. No matter how beneficial the result to the larger society, you are likely to feel unjustly treated.

It is difficult to argue with the proposition that a government contract or grant is a privilege which we can and should reserve for those who can demonstrate that they do not discriminate. Technically, that is all that the law requires, and if affirmative action programs actually worked that way, there would be no need for this discussion. But the requirements of the law and the realities of the marketplace are not the same thing, and intellectual honesty requires us to analyze what really happens—not what we think should happen.

Affirmative action laws do not require employers to hire persons who are not qualified. But as William Henry has pointed out in his recent book, *In Defense of Elitism,* those rules begin with the largely unexamined

premise that "fair" competition would automatically result in demographically proportional results.[1] Any deviation from the expected demographics—the so-called
utilization tables—is ipso facto proof of bias, or at the
very least, sufficient reason to shift the burden of
proving good faith to the employer. An employer whose
workforce varies from the relevant demographic pool
must justify that deviation.

Compliance with the reporting requirements imposed under affirmative action programs is costly and
time-consuming. If an audit of one's performance is required, that is more burdensome still. An employer is
far more likely to be audited if the percentages of
women and minorities employed are inconsistent with
government estimates of qualified persons in the target
groups. It is much easier simply to hire "by the numbers" than it is to justify the disparity. The result is
that many employers have de facto differences in qualifications for minority and nonminority employees—
and those differences do not go unnoticed by the employees involved.

Defenders of race-conscious government programs
argue that the results justify them. The barriers faced
by women and minorities were very real, and the numbers certainly demonstrate that we have expanded
their opportunities for education, employment, and ad-
vancement. The reporting process, while onerous, has
made employers think through the skills truly relevant
to a given job, and the additional clarity probably benefits everyone in the labor pool. If one accepts that
these are good outcomes (and I do), why should a
policy of minority preference bother us? If these programs, in practice, have operated to advantage members of groups who were previously disadvantaged, is
that so terrible? Haven't legal and social institutions

given white males undue advantage for generations? Those advantages were not based on "merit"—they were based upon skin color and prejudice. So why isn't turn-around (at least for a time) fair play?

The answer is that the prior acts of discrimination, widespread and accepted as they were, nevertheless constituted, and were seen as, departures from fundamental American beliefs about liberty and equality. The civil rights movement spoke to this nation with great moral force precisely because we knew that institutionalized racism was contrary to principles which form the bedrock of our constitutional system.

Government-mandated affirmative action is a deliberate deviation from those same principles in the name of a more compelling purpose. It is based upon the conviction that the ends justify the means. But our entire legal system is based on the belief that the ends do not justify the means. In our system, Hollywood notwithstanding, Dirty Harry is not justified in violating the rights of citizens, even guilty citizens. *In our system, the means are the ends.* The integrity of the process, the even-handedness of the law, is what civil liberties are all about.

Government mandates of inclusion based upon race or gender arouse opposition in large part because such programs are seen as contrary to fundamental civil liberties principles. When we have been truest to the American ideal, we have rejected categorizing people on the basis of qualities that ought to be legally irrelevant: race, religion, gender, disability, ethnicity. We do not recognize group rights in America—we recognize the rights of individuals, irrespective of their group affiliations. When we deviate from that principle, no matter how great the good we hope to accomplish, no matter how awful the injustice we seek to remedy, we send the

wrong signal. We encourage people to define themselves first as members of a particular group and only
then as members of the larger polity. Worse, we increase social polarization and feed group resentments
as Hispanics, Asians, women, the disabled, and count-
less others argue for proportional representation.

This is not to say that definable groups can never
receive special treatment. In a very compelling essay,
"The Legacy of Racial Injustice," Ira Glasser pointed to
various preferences given to veterans as an example of
a remedial program supposedly similar to affirmative
action.[2] But there is a crucial distinction: Entitlement
to a veteran's preference is based upon behavior, not
race or gender. Rewarding or punishing *behavior* is entirely consistent with civil liberties principles; rewarding or punishing *identity* is not. (The insistence by
gay activists on the term "sexual orientation" rather
than "sexual preference" is a tacit recognition of the
importance of this distinction. If being gay is an identity rather than a behavior, discrimination is improper.)
Those of us who believe that it is profoundly immoral
to disadvantage someone on the basis of skin color or
sex find it morally and intellectually inconsistent to
award advantage on that same basis. Doing so leads to
a sort of cognitive dissonance. We either follow our own
rules, or we don't. If we claim an exemption from those
rules based upon a higher moral purpose, how do we
distinguish ourselves from those who believe that a
"higher purpose" justifies suppressing pornography or
killing abortion doctors? Because "we" are right and
"they" are wrong?

I recently had lunch with a woman whom I have
known for years. She is not remotely a bigot; indeed, I
would count her as sensitive, thoughtful, and bright.
She is an opinion leader in our community. She is also

the mother of a son whose grades were good, but not quite good enough to gain him admittance to the competitive college that was his first choice. His mother sees her son as a white male victim of a system that allocates slots on the basis of race and sex rather than "merit."

I do not share this story because I agree with her; I don't. College admissions, particularly to private schools, have always been based upon a wide variety of factors other than merit—and "merit" is not necessarily calculated by adding grade point averages and test scores. I share this story because it demonstrates how corrosive the perception of preference has become.

That affirmative action (both the reality and the mythology) has engendered enormous backlash and ill will can hardly be denied. After some decades of progress, we are regressing into a more balkanized, more hyphenated Americanism. That cannot all be laid at the door of affirmative action programs—but they are clearly implicated. The resentments and hostilities are fact; any "letters to the editor" column will confirm their force. Much of the rhetoric is unfair, untrue, and based upon outright bigotry, but it resonates because the preferences it attacks are based upon special pleading and the politics of race. The acrimony is poisoning public discourse on these issues.

The one thing virtually all of us will agree upon is that our goal is the establishment of a society in which skin color, gender, and the like are absolutely irrelevant. Whether one is a proponent or a good-faith opponent of government-mandated affirmative action programs, most of us really do want a society where people are judged by their actions, their talents, and "the content of their character." I am compelled to conclude that legally mandated inclusion is not moving us toward that goal. It may have been expedient at one point, to force breaks with long-standing habits grounded in racism, to move people into jobs and educational institutions. But the time has come to ask whether those who are benefitting from government mandates today are even the people who need our help. More to the point, if these programs are now counterproductive, what shall we do instead?

In *Paved with Good Intentions: The Failure of Race Relations in Contemporary America,* Jared Taylor cites statistics for the proposition that blacks and whites with similar backgrounds and educations show no difference in average income.[3] Whatever the validity of that assertion, even the most ardent proponents of continued legal mandates will concede that poverty and hopelessness are greater barriers to equality than is race, and when coupled with race become even more so.

When I first began the practice of law, a partner in the firm told me that there is really only one legal question: What do we do? If we believe that the ends do not justify the means, that governmental distinctions based upon race are illegitimate no matter how benign the intent, what do we do instead? The answer to that question is really "where the rubber meets the road." Proponents of current law are entitled to question the motives of those who would dismantle current affirmative action programs without specifying what they propose as an alternative. When the right wing of my party objects to "reverse discrimination" without suggesting steps to eradicate discrimination against African-American and other historically disadvantaged groups, it rings a bit hollow.

If we are to move beyond affirmative action, we need to be very clear about what that means. It would be tragic if a change in approach were to be seen as a retreat from our national commitment to make amends for wrongs done and to repair, insofar as humanly possible, the damage inflicted by racism. We must continue to give courts the tools to fashion remedies in cases where discrimination has been demonstrated. We must also provide additional resources to state and local civil rights commissions, to allow prompt, thorough investigation of alleged discriminatory behavior. Many, perhaps most, such agencies are woefully underfunded; in some jurisdictions, cases languish for years. In short, we need to make nondiscrimination a genuinely high priority, not merely a pious exhortation or a code for maintaining the status quo.

We should also be prepared to replace efforts based on race and gender with programs for the economically disadvantaged. Socioeconomic factors divide people more profoundly than racial ones. In our guilty emphasis on skin color, we have contributed to a mythology that interferes with our ability to see similarities across racial lines. I have more in common with an African-American lawyer than with a Caucasian short-order cook. There are innumerable ways to categorize citizens that do not depend upon immutable characteristics. We need to fashion programs that will help people who need help. Race and gender are no longer reliable predictors of who those people are—and that, at least, is progress. The challenge is to devise criteria for assistance that do not contribute to further polarization.

Kenneth Clark is a well-known social psychologist whose work on the self-esteem of black children was an important part of the record in *Brown* v. *Board of Education,* the 1954 landmark case ending legal school segregation in America. In an interview with Sam Barber in the *New York Times,* Clark reiterated his lifelong commitment to integration. Asked whether blacks still need preferential treatment, he replied "I don't believe in preferential treatment. To me, that is a form of racism." Kenneth Clark is exactly right. Let us by all means take vigorous affirmative steps to abolish racism, which is still epidemic in this country. But let us resist the patronizing impulse to simply substitute a "kinder, gentler" version for the older model.

NOTES

1. William Henry, *In Defense of Elitism* (New York: Doubleday, 1994).

2. Ira Glasser, "The Legacy of Racial Injustice," *Common Ground* 1, no. 2 (Winter 1995).

3. Jared Taylor, *Paved with Good Intentions: The Failure of Race Relations in Contemporary America* (New York: Carrol & Graf, 1993).

12

What Did You Learn in School Today?

★★

My guess is that the ACLU is about as popular among public school officials as that proverbial IRS agent—the one who says "I'm from the government and I'm here to help you." The ACLU is the source of innumerable headaches for school administrations. But it is a love/hate relationship.

Almost everyone has said to a child, at one time or another, something like "If I didn't care about you, I wouldn't care what you do. I wouldn't care if you learned to follow the rules." The same thing is true of the ACLU's relationship with the public schools. As often as we may be pains in their posteriors, as often as we engage in debates about random drug testing or censoring T-shirts or high school newspapers, civil libertarians are absolutely committed to the institution of public education. We recognize, as too many do not, that public schools—good public schools, supported by their communities—are an essential ingredient of a democratic society.

Why would a libertarian Republican support *any* bureaucracy, let alone the undeniably bureaucratic public school system? If markets are good, should there not be a marketplace for education? If the power of the state is to be restrained, why in the world would we give government a monopoly to shape the minds and characters of the nation's children? What power could be greater—and potentially more threatening— than the indoctrination of the young?

If attendance at government schools were mandatory, I would agree. But the constitution protects those who wish to remove their children from the state's schools. Parents may send their children to private or parochial schools, or they may home school, and the state cannot object. America has always had "school choice." The issue being debated in communities today is not whether choice shall exist; it is about whether public schools will continue to exist.

One of the core beliefs that drew me to the Republican party was the ideal of equality of opportunity. Equality of opportunity is diametrically opposed to egalitarianism, or equality of results. When I first became politically active, the distinction between the two was essentially the distinction between Republicans and Democrats; we Republicans believed in creating an environment which enabled and rewarded merit and hard work, while (it seemed to me, at least) the Democrats were more interested in redistribution—ensuring a minimum *result* for everyone, irrespective of effort. While I was perfectly willing to concede that letting people starve in the streets was both unkind and unwise, I believed then and I believe now that our efforts ought to be targeted to ensuring every citizen an equal place at the starting line, and rewards roughly commensurate with the market value of the subsequent performance.

It is impossible to be genuinely committed to such a system without also committing to those measures required to create a "level playing field." One of the reasons so many people view Republicans as mean-spirited today is that they see a lot of *rhetoric* about equal opportunity and merit as a basis for reward, but they don't see those who are employing that rhetoric following its logic. If people are subject to job discrimination because their skin is a different color, or their sexual orientation is deemed abnormal; if still other people do not have the economic means to acquire basic skills needed to enter the job market; then we don't have equal opportunity. People will always vary in their intelligence, diligence, and skills; those of us who believe in the market economy have made a determination that we all benefit when more productive people get bigger rewards. We are willing to live with that kind of inequality, because a rising tide really does lift all boats. An economy that rewards achievement is better even for the nonachievers. Rather than cutting the existing pie into ever smaller bits, we opt for a system likely to produce bigger pies. But the inequality we are prepared to accept cannot—morally, economically, or practically—be built on structural inequity, on the uneven playing field. It cannot be built upon inequality of *opportunity.*

America supports universal publicly funded education so that the children of the poor and uneducated, the children of immigrants, orphans, and others will have access to the same intellectual tools as children from more fortunate families. Schools are a necessary condition to the enduring American belief that—with hard work, grit, and just a little luck—any youngster can grow up to be president. Colin Powell strikes such a chord with most of us because he embodies and confirms that belief. (Powell, a poor black child born to immigrant parents, grew up to become the immensely popular Chairman of the Joint Chiefs of Staff and the object of an intense "draft Powell" effort by voters in both parties who wanted him to undertake an independent run for the presidency.) Public schools are necessary if we truly mean to construct a society in which everyone, not just the fortunate, can participate.

There is another element to the Republican commitment to equal opportunity: a belief in the importance of standards. Frequently, this belief is dismissed as elitist, but in fact it is anything but. If Americans are to be trusted to govern ourselves, there are certain standards we must meet, citizenship skills we must acquire, a common vocabulary we must learn. We have built an entire legal system on the assumption that all Americans can learn to participate in the great adventure of self-government. Public schools are where we teach future citizens public virtues. They are as necessary to our philosophical construct as roads and sewers are to the built environment.

Those who advocate for vouchers and similar programs will concede each of those points. However, they say, all of these goals can be achieved without government-operated schools. If government simply pays for the schooling, it is by their definition sufficiently "public." Poor children will still receive an education— and in many instances, an education superior to what they are getting now. Simply give parents a voucher representing a certain number of tax dollars for each school-age child and let the parent decide where to "spend" the money. The market will provide choices based upon the desires of these "consumers."

There are many reasons why the superficial lure of vouchers proves ephemeral upon closer examination.

Such systems will not—cannot—live up to the promises made by their partisans, but that is not the reason I oppose them. Tax dollars cannot constitutionally go to parochial schools, but even that is not the most fundamental objection.

We depend upon our public—yes, our *government*—schools to transmit the core civic values that are or should be common to the entire American community. A great deal is being written today about American culture, most of it ethnocentric nonsense, but that does not mean there is no such thing as a distinctive American ethic. The job for our schools is to teach the values that are fundamental to that ethic and thereby to support and strengthen the American community.

Government schools are engaged in transmitting widely held American standards of civic and cultural literacy. Private schools may or may not do so; being private, they are entitled to reflect the desires and needs of their sponsors. By definition, they serve specialized constituencies—they need not be accredited, need not teach any generally accepted dogmas; they need not even teach in the English language, for that matter. Because the government does not fund them, it does not direct their activities or dictate their curricula. Private schools today offer a real choice to the relative few who choose them, precisely because they are not subject to government control. Because the great preponderance of America's students are in state schools, the existence of these nonconforming institutions does not threaten the transmission of the culture—rather, it provides a leavening and corrective agent for the inevitable problems citizens will experience with any monopoly.

If tax dollars flow to nonpublic schools, the initial effect will be fragmentation and grossly uneven results. Ironically, the end result would likely be a new public school system; legislators are generally (and properly) unwilling to allocate tax dollars without strings attached. Furthermore, as a citizen, if my tax dollars are going to the XYZ School, I want to know that it is teaching math and English—that my taxes are not supporting a school for smelling flowers or contacting extraterrestrials. If I am African-American and my tax dollars are supporting the local segregation academy or the Ku Klux Klan preschool, I'm likely to be unhappy. Privately funded choice programs can work because they *are* private. The minute tax dollars are involved, however, the fiduciary duty of legislators trumps the First Amendment rights of the schools receiving support. Schools wishing to partake of public funding will have to meet government standards.

Government-run public schools are one of the few remaining "street corners" in an increasingly balkanized society. They are part of an endangered social infrastructure that promotes our shared identity as Americans. We no longer live (if we ever did) in a society where Mom meets with the ladies at the Garden Club, while Dad discusses the latest "Fugitive" episode with the guys at the office water cooler. Whether those times were really better, as so many of the social revisionists claim (and I doubt), there is no bringing them back. I would wager that is true in even the smallest, most traditional of communities. In a country where the things that divide us vastly outnumber the things that bring us together, the public schools really do become our "street corner," our common ground.

Public schools are the mechanism through which we inculcate our national values—and make no mistake, the transmission of those values is not only constitutionally permissible, it is inescapable. There is no such thing as value-neutral education. When schools are attacked for failing to teach values, the real complaint is that we are not teaching the particular values deemed appropriate by the folks who are doing the complaining.

We cannot teach sectarian religious beliefs in our public schools. We are forbidden from doing so by the First Amendment, and even if that were not so, the diversity of America would make it impossible. But we certainly can—and do—transmit the essential principles that underlie our representative democracy. In a wonderful essay in *Harper's Magazine* sometime back, called "America Skips School," Benjamin Barber wrote:

> We have forgotten that the "public" in public schools means not just paid for by the public but procreative of the very idea of a public. Public schools are how a public—a citizenry—is forged and how young, selfish individuals turn into conscientious, community-minded citizens.
>
> Among the several literacies that have attracted the anxious attention of commentators, civil literacy has been the least visible. Yet this is the fundamental literacy by which we live in a civil society. It encompasses the competence to participate in democratic communities, the ability to think critically and act with deliberation in a pluralistic world, and the empathy to identify sufficiently with others to live with them despite conflicts of interest and differences in character. At the most elementary level, what our children suffer from most, whether they're hurling racial epithets from fraternity porches or shooting one another down in schoolyards, is the absence of civility.
>
> Civility is a work of the imagination, for it is through the imagination that we render others sufficiently like ourselves for them to become subjects of

tolerance and respect, if not always affection. Democracy is anything but a "natural" form of association. It is an extraordinary and rare contrivance of cultivated imagination. Give the uneducated the right to participate in making collective decisions, and what results is not democracy but, at best, mob rule: the government of private prejudice once known as the tyranny of opinion. For Jefferson, the difference between the democratic temperance he admired in agrarian America and the rule of the rabble he condemned when viewing the social unrest of Europe's teeming cities was quite simply education. Madison had hoped to "filter" out popular passion through the device of representation. Jefferson saw in education a filter that could be installed within each individual, giving to each the capacity to rule prudently. Education creates a ruling aristocracy constrained by temperance and wisdom; when that education is public and universal, it is an aristocracy to which all can belong. At its best, the American dream of a free and equal society governed by judicious citizens has been this dream of an aristocracy of everyone.[1]

If one agrees with Barber that public education thus defined is one of our most important civic responsibilities, how do we account for the absolute ferocity and mean-spiritedness of current attacks on that institution?

I am not referring here to legitimate concerns voiced by businesses who want a more dependable supply of skilled workers. I am not talking about philosophical debates over mainstreaming, or educational programs for gifted students, or the merits of standardized testing. And I am certainly not suggesting that failing schools should not be a cause of great concern. I am talking about the attacks (admittedly originating at the far fringes of the political spectrum) on the very idea of public education—attacks that demonize educators, distort facts, and are anything but civil. Let me share just a few quotations from speakers at the 1995 summer convention of the Christian Coalition. According to a report in the October 1995 issue of *Church and State,* a magazine published by Americans United for Separation of Church and State, "speaker after speaker railed against Supreme Court decisions upholding church-state separation, demanded voucher subsidies for private religious schooling, and bashed the public school system, the U. S. Department of Education, and the NEA."

Pat Buchanan criticized public schools, charging that "God and the Bible have been replaced with *Playboy* and condoms. We don't need some miserable secular humanist in sandals and beads at the Department of Education telling us how to educate American's children." And another popular speaker, Star Parker, an antiwelfare activist, said, "You want to solve the education crisis? Then get the government out of it. Privatize it—100 percent. I'm serious. Oh, you can't find a school? Oh, we abolished all your schools? Then home school. Teach your kids at home." She added that parents could give their children better instruction "in a shed" if they had to.

During a breakout session titled "Elementary School Curriculum [*sic*]: Are We Dumbing Down America?" Ezola Foster, founder of a group called Americans for Family Values, said public schools have gone from "academic learning centers to socialist training camps."

Let me be very clear on this: the ICLU would sue to protect an individual parent's right to "opt out" of the system, for religious or any other reasons. Parents

have a right to raise their own children as they see fit.
Nor am I making the "Pollyanna" argument that all is
well in all of our public schools or that schools cannot
be the subject of criticism. But in many cases, the
schools are simply a convenient scapegoat, blamed for
conditions beyond their control.

When I was in high school—back in the dark ages—
students who weren't on what was then called the "academic track" (i.e., college bound) went to work in local
factories, where the skills required were relatively min-
imal and the pay was sufficient to maintain a middle-
class lifestyle. Those jobs aren't there any longer. In a
speech several years ago, Albert Shanker* said that in
his youth, America educated around 25 percent of the
students who came through the system; today, we are
still educating about 25 percent—but there are no longer
easily available jobs for the uneducated 75 percent.

While the 1950s were hardly the paradigm of social
bliss portrayed by some folks with selective memories,
it is certainly true that most city schools did not have
to cope with widespread drug use, or as high an incidence of broken homes, or student turnover rates that
exceed 200 percent in some urban areas. (Test scores
aren't very meaningful when the kids you test at the
beginning of the year aren't the same ones you test at
the end.) The diversity that characterizes classrooms
even in smaller, more rural communities was inconceivable even a decade ago. America is also educating
a larger percentage of the school-age population.
(Mandatory attendance laws have been beefed up in
many states and the age for legally quitting school has

---

*Shanker is past president of the American Federation of
Teachers. He writes a weekly column on education called "Where
I Stand" for the Sunday *New York Times*.

been raised. More important, fewer kids drop out immediately upon becoming old enough to quit.) Despite all this, and contrary to the negative rhetoric, real achievement levels have held steady or risen in most school systems. In the face of formidable challenges, public schools have performed remarkably well.

I found it particularly interesting that when *Money* magazine—hardly an organ of the National Education Association—did a study of public and private schools in October 1994, it concluded that public schools were a better value. Specifically, the study found:

- Students who attend the best public schools outperform most private school students.

- The average public school teacher has stronger academic qualifications than the average private school teacher.

- The best public schools offer a more challenging curriculum than most private schools.

- Public school class sizes are no larger than in most private schools and are smaller than in most Catholic schools.[2]

The editors admitted that the results "shocked" them—many of them sent their own children to private schools and all of them began by assuming that the facts would favor private schools. When they looked at the *evidence*, however, rather than the rhetoric, they concluded that most public schools do a very good job.

And while the prose was a bit hysterical and the general tone overly defensive, a recent book by David C. Berliner and Bruce J. Biddle—*The Manufactured Crisis*—does a good job of looking behind the sound bytes and at the evidence of public school performance, which they find generally positive.[3] Their most important contribution, I thought, was to highlight the vast differences that exist within the public school system from state to state. Some schools perform abysmally—many more do an excellent job. In view of such differences, they point out, discussions of "average" performance are meaningless—sort of like trying to "average" an elephant and a mouse. The result doesn't describe either one.

If public schools vary widely in performance, and if the majority are really doing a reasonably good job, how do we account for the unrelenting war that has been waged on them the past few years?

I am convinced that the great preponderance of attacks on public education are part and parcel of today's culture wars. Attacks on the schools have become an ideological tool in a high stakes game of power politics. The public schools have become a convenient target for extremist political groups, *precisely because the schools are so important—and effective—in transmitting our national values.*

If schools teach the value of freedom of expression, how will we rid the libraries and airwaves of material we find objectionable? If schools teach that all citizens are entitled to equal treatment before the law, how can we be sure that children will grow up to condemn gays and lesbians? How can we ensure that women will understand their obligation to be submissive to their husbands? If schools teach that religious liberty requires government neutrality, how will we signal the superiority of the "Judeo-Christian tradition?" What if children grow up believing in evolution? In the separation of church and state? If schools teach that the Constitution protects a zone of privacy, will women think they can make their own decisions about procreation and reproduction? If we can't make children pray in school, how can we even be sure that they are praying to the right God? Or praying at all?

Obviously, if America is to experience the spiritual transformation so earnestly desired by these groups, the public schools will have to go.

School administrators today are really in an unenviable situation. Every day, in addition to everything else they must do, they must strike the proper balance between the rights of individual children and their parents, on the one hand, and their responsibility to transmit fundamental tenets of American representative democracy on the other. Inevitably, some of them strike that balance in ways we at the ICLU believe to be unwarranted, and when they do, they hear from us. But they hear from us because we understand that what they do, and how they do it, is critically important. In a very real sense, the fate of the American experiment with liberty rests with the institution of public education. If we abandon it, rather than working to fix it, we will be abandoning the quintessentially American belief that anyone, from any background, can succeed. We will also be abandoning our single most effective mechanism for creating out of our diversity a community of citizens with shared civic values. Public schools were intended to be the great equalizers, the institutions that would assure all America's children of an equal place at the starting line. They are the visible evidence of our commitment to equal opportunity, and for that reason they are irreplaceable.

NOTES

1. Benjamin Barber, "America Skips School," *Harper's Magazine* (November 1993).

2. *Money* (October 1994).

3. David C. Berliner and Bruce J. Biddle, *The Manufactured Crisis: Myths, Fraud, and the Attack on America's Public Schools* (Reading, Mass.: Addison-Wesley, 1995).

13

Keeping Civil Tongues
in Our Heads

★★

A liberal friend of mine recently wondered about the identity of those groups Pat Robertson is always talking about —the ones whose mission is the destruction of the American family. I immediately imagined the meetings of such organizations: "Aha!" one member might chortle, "I got the local school to promote promiscuity in sex education." "I did better than that," another might respond. "I lined the kids up and had them spit on the American flag."

Does any sane participant in public debate truly believe that "they" (whoever "they" may be) are consciously and deliberately setting out to do *harm*? If not, how do we account for the nastiness that passes for public rhetoric?

I have read enough history to know that the art of invective wasn't invented by Pat Buchanan and his ilk. When Thomas Jefferson was running for president, newspapers of the day predicted the wholesale burning of Bibles if such a godless politician were to be elected. Our

157

collective fascination with the sex lives of our presidents goes back at least as far as Grover Cleveland (1885–1889), who was the subject of a rhyme about his alleged illegitimate child: "Ma, ma, where's my pa? Gone to the White House, haw haw haw" (poetry wasn't their long suit). I am not about to endorse speech codes—as a civil libertarian, I oppose attempts by government to limit even the most hateful speech. Being opposed to censorship, however, does not equate to approval of what all people may be saying. The principles of the First Amendment prohibit my interference with the free speech rights of others; the responsibilities of citizenship require my active response to both the content and tone of the messages I hear.

Today, we face unprecedented economic change—global in scope, but increasingly local in effect. Advances in science are presenting us with new and thorny ethical issues. The omnipresence of the media, the proliferation of channels through which we have virtually instantaneous worldwide communication, has created an entirely new and potentially overwhelming political environment. If we are going to navigate these changes successfully, we are going to have to begin by recognizing that those with whom we disagree are generally well-meaning, and by remembering that they have as much right to their opinions as we have to ours. As distasteful as it may seem to those who pride themselves on ideological purity, it is both necessary and possible to find common ground with people with whom we disagree; possible to have productive exchanges without one side winning and one losing. There is more to public debate than scoring points.

For the past couple of years, I have carried on a sporadic correspondence with a woman I have never met. She began our exchange by sending me a copy of the prolife newsletter she edits, together with a brief note sharing her horror and dismay over the murder of a doctor who performed abortions. She wanted me and other prochoice activists to understand that such acts cannot reflect the views of truly *prolife* people, by definition. Subsequent correspondence has revealed a common concern for the free speech rights of abortion protesters. We both worry that government is using RICO laws* to stifle dissent. While we will never agree on the central issue, the right of government to interfere with a woman's reproductive decisions, I respect her sincerity and her willingness to work within the system to change what she cannot accept. She respects my right to hold a different view. And on at least one occasion, we both had letters in a northern Indiana newspaper arguing that violence against abortion providers and infringement of protesters' First Amendment rights are both wrong. She does not consider me a murderous antichrist and I do not believe she is motivated by a desire to oppress women. We simply hold opposing positions on an important public issue. We have chosen to engage in *civil discourse*—and we have both "won," even though neither of us has been persuaded by the other— because we have avoided becoming culture warriors.

The term "culture wars" was coined by James D. Hunter, who addressed divisions of opinion on the so-called social issues in a book called *Culture Wars: The Struggle to Define America.*[1] Hunter argued that the culture wars have their foundation in "a profound realignment in American culture which cuts across established

---

*RICO is the acronym for the Racketeer Influenced and Corrupt Organizations Act of 1970. Originally intended as a weapon against organized crime, RICO has been used against abortion clinic protesters and "dirty" bookstores; prosecutors have been increasingly creative in devising arguments to expand the use of RICO far beyond the original Congressional intent.

moral and religious communities." He described a growing alliance among Christian fundamentalists, Orthodox
Jews, and conservative Catholics to do battle against
their progressive counterparts—secularists, reform
Jews, liberal Catholics, and mainstream Protestants.

Anyone engaged in the battle for reproductive choice,
gay rights, or intellectual freedom can confirm the accuracy of Hunter's observations. Our challenge is to focus
the inevitable debates on our ideological differences, to
attack ideas rather than people. It will not be easy.

Recently, I came across a newspaper produced and
distributed by a group of fundamentalist churches in
northern Indiana. The publication hits every hot but-
ton described by Hunter. Family values are "real"
Christian values, certainly not those espoused by
mainline denominations with their suspect "liberal" in-
terpretations of biblical truth. Homosexuals were the
menace of choice. All homosexuals, the paper reports,
have hundreds of sex partners each year and prey
upon young people in order to convert them to this
"ungodly lifestyle." Abortion is murder, and those who
have harmed doctors and clinics are simply acting on
the biblical principle of an eye for an eye. Pornography—including much of contemporary television programming—is being used by Satan and the secular humanists to destroy the moral fiber of the country. And
so on. There is no attempt to distinguish between the
"sin" and the "sinner" in order to hate the one and love
the other. Those who deviate from correct beliefs are
not portrayed as merely wrong—they are evil.

I would like to dismiss such rhetoric as the product
of a small number of terribly frightened people, which it
surely is. But anyone who has watched the (marginally)
smoother version of all this on the "700 Club" and its
clones, or on Rush Limbaugh and his, can attest to the

money and power being generated by those who es-
pouse such views. Their growing influence does not
bode well for the democratic process. People who believe
God wants all faggots stoned to death are not open to
dialogue and negotiation. People who are convinced
that God wants doctors who perform abortions shot to
death in the name of life are immune to discussions of
religious pluralism and the constitutional right to self-
determination. People so fearful of the power of ideas
that they try to ban books and television programs are
unlikely to be receptive to alternative points of view.

It has been my experience that zealots are more likely
to participate in political activities than are moderates.
True believers—unhindered by doubt or second thoughts
and strangers to moral ambiguity—have an overwhelming need to impose their vision of righteousness and sal-
vation on the rest of us. It goes without saying that these
culture warriors have every right to proclaim their views
in the public square. The threat comes when more reasonable voices cede the political process to them, leaving
us with an impoverished and polarizing political language void of nuance or complexity.

In 1994, the Indiana Civil Liberties Union launched
what I then called a "Campaign for Civility." It was generated by my frustration with the increasing nastiness
of public rhetoric, and my conviction that it required
some sort of response. In the six-month period pre-
ceding the campaign, I had received letters or literature
containing each of the following statements:

> Homosexuals engage in practices so vile, foul, and
> rotten they cannot be printed in the paper . . .

> The radical feminist group wants to control our gov-
> ernment through threat and manipulation, to attack
> the Bible-believing church, and to bring witchcraft

and the occult, specifically goddess worship, to the women of America.

In 1960 America elected its first and only Roman Catholic into office. The event was the nemesis of American government . . .

This [an ICLU lawsuit] is an attack on Christians . . . the ACLU is 95% Jewish.

While these examples are admittedly from the far fringes of the political spectrum, name calling and demonization have increasingly moved into the mainstream. In the "culture war," language has become a casualty of ideology. Perfectly good phrases have been transformed into code words. Thus, on the right, "media elite" has become a negative reference to Jews; "family values" a shorthand for adherence to fundamentalist Christian ideology. On the left, "right-wing fundamentalist" is frequently used to mean intolerant and anti-intellectual. It is seductively simple: once we have reduced a complex issue to a slogan suitable for bumper stickers; once we have reduced a group of human beings to stereotypes, we no longer have to deal with that issue or negotiate with those beings.

Most Americans are not haters. Polls and surveys confirm that while mean-spirited rhetoric may rally the troops of true believers, it repels the vast majority of less ideological folk. Unfortunately, those polls and surveys also confirm what political observers have predicted for the last several years: as the level of public meanness rises, the level of public participation falls. Rather than become involved with an enterprise increasingly seen as shoddy and unproductive, large numbers of Americans have simply tuned out.

We can't talk to each other if we don't listen to each

other—and a working democracy requires that citizens engage in real dialogue rather than the exchange of sound bytes. There have always been shrill and angry participants in public debate, but they have been balanced by the active engagement of their more temperate fellows. Today, the voices of moderation are deserting the field. In the past several months, members of Congress noted for courtesy and collegiality have left Washington in droves. Those who elect to remain have adopted a meaner tone. This continuing debasement of public rhetoric has ominous implications. As I wrote our members, "The civil liberties we cherish are dependent for their continued existence on mutually respectful, thoughtful discourse; dependent upon the premise that one can be steadfast without being shrill, disapproving of someone else's behavior or legal position without being vitriolic, hateful, or intellectually dishonest. For some, obviously, the ends justify the means—but for us, for civil libertarians, the ends *are* the means: the integrity of the political process and the marketplace of ideas."

The "Campaign for Civility" emphasized the importance of courtesy and mutual respect in the face of deeply held differences of opinion. As I told my members, I was under no delusion that we would somehow be able to turn the spigot and stop the flow of vitriol and ugliness. But we could refuse to participate. We could resolve to use our free speech rights to persuade others of the need for civil discourse.

While the overwhelming majority of those who responded to the Campaign endorsed the need to encourage civil and thoughtful discussion, there were some who were clearly uncomfortable with the notion of the ACLU urging verbal restraint. One of my board members expressed his concern that the effort smacked of "political correctness." Another suggested

that such a campaign was inconsistent with adherence
to the principle of free speech.

There are clearly those who do not believe that courtesy and intellectual passion can coexist. This may explain a comment made to me by the executive director of
an organization whose board I had joined a few months
earlier. He confessed that he had expected the head of
the ICLU to be "mean," and he was pleasantly surprised
that I wasn't. I assured him that it is perfectly possible to
believe in the Bill of Rights without being grim, but I certainly understood how his expectations had been
shaped. Today, the very word "advocate" conjures up the
image of a humorless, rigid, and self-righteous shrew. In
this, at least, left and right, totalitarian and libertarian
are truly indistinguishable. Direct mail campaigns by the
ACLU aren't much different than those conducted by the
Christian Coalition or the Republican National Committee. Only the enemy has been changed. Such appeals
may fill organizational treasuries, but they do a serious
disservice to public dialogue. Worse, as the public becomes more sophisticated, they contribute to a dangerous and growing cynicism about American institutions.

Has the American political process gotten to the point
where an endorsement of civility is controversial? Is contemporary political rhetoric so driven by the imperative
of the sound byte that genuine public dialogue is no
longer possible? Have political extremists succeeded in
making "tolerance" a bad word? Is it possible that I
cannot be an effective advocate for civil liberties unless I
am confrontational and unkind? If so, what does all this
say about the prospects for American democracy?

We cannot find common ground without civility and
we cannot solve our problems without finding common
ground. Unless those of us who believe in the American
experiment step up to counter those on the left and

right who are preaching hate and division, our ability to continue the American experiment will be compromised—perhaps fatally. Whether the Buchanans and Limbaughs approve or not, America is the most diverse nation on earth. We are black, brown, white, and yellow; Jewish, Hindu, Muslim, Christian, and atheist; rich, middle class, and poor. We are educated and ignorant, Republican and Democrat, straight and gay, urban and rural. Unlike societies based upon the homogeneity of populations, we are held together by an idea—a unique philosophy of governance. It requires a great deal of us as citizens, including at an absolute minimum that we handle our inevitable differences with courtesy and mutual respect. Civility is an essential condition of our *civitas.*

We cannot allow the fanatics and zealots to capture the political process and monopolize the public debate.

We cannot allow the democratic process to become a casualty of the culture wars.

The Talmud says you are not expected to change the world in one generation, but you are not free not to try. We can't change the fact that many people will act out of fright, anger, and hate, but we can redouble our own efforts to foster thoughtful and meaningful discussion. We can refuse to engage in the culture wars. We can contribute to a principled public dialogue. We can embrace and defend the principles embodied in the Declaration of Independence, the Constitution, and the Bill of Rights. We can try.

And we must.

NOTE

1. James D. Hunter, *Culture Wars: The Struggle to Define America* (New York: Basic Books, 1991).

14

It's a Crummy Job, But Someone Has to Do It

★★

I have a dirty little secret. Several, actually. I don't care very much about the rights of prisoners. I think school uniforms are probably a pretty good idea. And I was *glad* when the police officers who beat Rodney King were retried after a trial I considered a travesty. Sometimes, I get tired of standing on principle. By nature, I am a person who would rather compromise with you than draw a line in the sand and dare you to cross it.

So what in the world am I doing at the ACLU, defending prisoners' rights, opposing school uniforms, insisting that double jeopardy means what it says— daily drawing lines in the sand?

I am at the ACLU because *someone has to do it*. Not long ago, a television reporter in our city was doing a series on prisoner lawsuits. He had numerous examples of genuinely ridiculous claims. He had come to me for a quote or two on why these suits weren't as dumb as they seemed, and why we shouldn't move to cut them off. But he was asking the wrong question. The suits in his examples were every bit as dumb as they seemed—and if there were a way to cut them off without also cutting off the small percentage of meritorious complaints, I would endorse doing so. The real question is this: Are we willing, as a society, to wade through a lot of frivolous nonsense in order to prevent a few really horrible abuses? And the answer to *that* question must be yes. In my brief tenure with the ACLU, I have seen situations that truly shock the conscience: female prisoners raped by guards; a terminal AIDS patient told if he couldn't chew regular prison food he could starve; a seventeen-year-old boy (arrested for a $78 outstanding traffic ticket) beaten to death by other prisoners who had severely beaten another boy just days before.

For every complaint my office receives from a prisoner that has any merit at all, we get literally hundreds that are frivolous. But does anyone doubt for a minute that the real abuses would increase if no one were watching?

As I have said before, the Bill of Rights is not self-enforcing. The constitution of the Soviet Union had lots of nice language about individual rights, but that language was routinely ignored. The ACLU exists to be a pain in the ass; to remind lawmakers puffed up with their own importance that *we follow the rules here.* It is clearly not a job for folks who need to be popular.

When the ACLU was founded in 1920, citizens were being jailed for holding antiwar views. A U.S. attorney named J. Mitchell Palmer was conducting raids on resident aliens suspected of unorthodox beliefs (the "Red Scare"). Racial segregation was the law, and antiblack violence was widespread and condoned. That was the year women finally got the vote, but other forms of gender discrimination continued to flourish. And the Supreme Court of the United States had never upheld a single First Amendment free speech claim.

Cases brought by the ACLU have changed America, even the ones we didn't win. Everyone has heard about the 1925 *Scopes* trial, an ACLU challenge to a Tennessee statute forbidding the teaching of evolution; fewer recall that even with so distinguished a lawyer as Clarence Darrow, we lost that case and the law remained on the books until 1967. In 1933, we successfully battled the government's refusal to allow James Joyce's *Ulysses* to be sold in the United States. And in the long series of cases that have followed, ACLU lawyers established principles that we now take for granted: public places like streets and parks belong to the people, not the government; "separate but equal" isn't; the right to privacy includes a married couple's right to use contraception and a woman's right to choose; the government cannot forbid whites from marrying blacks; poor people cannot be prevented from traveling from state to state; the government cannot force children to salute the flag in violation of their religious beliefs; restrictive covenants barring blacks or Jews from residential subdivisions cannot be enforced; poor people charged with a crime have a right to a court-appointed lawyer; democracy means "one person, one vote." These and many other rules are taken for granted by citizens today, but each and every one of these rights was won in defiance of the conventional wisdom and majority opinion of the times.

It has been estimated that more than *80 percent* of the so-called landmark Supreme Court cases included in standard constitutional law textbooks involve the ACLU.

We may not always be right, but we are truly indispensable. A system constructed on an adversarial model—majoritarianism versus libertarianism—cannot achieve a proper balance unless the interests of both are vigorously, stubbornly, and persistently represented. In the nature of things, the majority will always exercise enormous power over the institutions of government. Unless there is a countervailing force to insist on the rights of the individual, the individual will not have rights.

When I was in private practice, I considered myself an advocate for my clients. It was my job to make each one's case as forcefully as possible. The lawyer on the other side was supposed to be making his or her client's case with equal force. That clash of positions sharpened the issues for resolution, whether through negotiation or litigation. Strenuous and emphatic arguments on behalf of differing interests were necessary to obtain a just result. Today, my "client" is the Bill of Rights, and my job is to advocate for the liberties protected by that document as forcefully as possible. It is the job of the government and its lawyers to justify existing or proposed infringements of those liberties, and the job of the courts to decide whose position will prevail.

The ACLU is often accused of "pushing the envelope," of working for the constant expansion of individual rights, even to the detriment of societal or communal interests. *That is our job.* It is the job of those who believe that a given expansion of rights is unwarranted or dangerous to make that case. Much of the annoyance with the ACLU comes from a misunderstanding of our role. We are liberty's lawyers, not society's.

As important as it is to enlarge liberty, to fight for new applications of constitutional principles, it is equally important that we defend the freedoms we have already won. As I am writing this, the ACLU has gone to court to challenge Congressional action censoring the Internet. A local columnist dismissed the effort with a statement scorning the ACLU's "tiresome arguments about free speech and privacy." Well, yes, I suppose we do get tiresome. But most of my clients have *wanted* a lawyer who will be eternally vigilant on their behalf. I cannot recall a single case where a client engaged my services with the statement, "Well, do what you can but don't represent me too vigorously." That columnist and many others have the luxury of being blasé about their rights precisely because the ACLU is not.

A few months ago our staff attorney told me about receiving a phone call from a lawyer whose client had been jailed in a nearby county. In jail with her client was a man who had been locked up for over forty-seven days without ever once being brought before a judge or anyone with authority to set bail or appoint counsel. Cheri called the prosecutor, who referred her to the county attorney. The next day, the man had his hearing.

No lawsuit. No public fulminations. Just a reminder to people who know that because we are prepared to be "tiresome," they had better be prepared to follow the rules. And the rules say the government can't simply lock people up indefinitely without a preliminary hearing. If this is someone who needs to be kept behind bars, the government has an obligation to demonstrate why.

My office makes similar calls every week. So do the other ACLU offices around the country. In large part, it is because we are there, because we are prepared to be "tiresome," that government follows the rules.

The real irony—and real testament to our mission—is that those who criticize us the loudest are the first to call upon us when *their* rights are violated. Whom did Oliver North call for help in securing his due process rights? The ACLU. Few groups can match the vitriol of the Christian Coalition when discussing the ACLU—yet when we join them in a case like *Lamb's Chapel*,* our participation is cited as evidence that their argument is sound. In our state, we often represent police officers—and even more often, get referrals from them. Despite the rhetoric of some in the Republican party, Republicans improperly fired by a Democratic administration called on us to vindicate their rights. If actions speak louder than words, such actions confirm the importance of what we do, and the even-handedness with which we do it.

Lamb's Chapel v. *Center Moriches Union Free School District* involved a school's refusal to allow use of its facilities by a church. The school routinely allowed community groups to use its facilities; the activity was not during school hours and was entirely voluntary. Both the ACLU and the ACLJ saw the refusal as improperly based upon the religious content of the program. In the absence of any governmental endorsement of religion, or coercion of students to attend, there was no reason to treat the church differently than any other community group.

15

Won't You Come Home, Barry Goldwater?

★★

Like many traditional Republicans, I have been alarmed and saddened by the ascendance of the radical right wing of my party.

Recently, I picked up an article that discussed GOP congressional priorities during 1995: repealing the assault weapons ban; returning prayer to the public schools; restricting access to abortion; outlawing flag burning; and keeping gays out of the military.

This is not the agenda of a party devoted to limiting the power of the state. With the sole exception of the gun issue, every single item on that Congressional agenda involved more government intrusion in our lives rather than less. And yet these were initiatives championed by people who asked for our votes in 1994 on the entirely reasonable grounds that we need to control the growth of government and roll back its influence in our lives. These are the same members of Congress who can be seen regularly on C-SPAN advocating for repeal of government regulations over our economic behaviors and advocating a "leaner, meaner" federal bureaucracy.

If I were a psychiatrist and my political party were my patient, the diagnosis would be schizophrenia.

In large part, the party has been captured by our extremists. These are the folks who—while relatively few in absolute numbers—have worked hard at the grassroots level in order to advance their particular theocratic agenda. While the rest of us have been sitting on our fannies, they have been organizing, fundraising, and running for political and public office. And their diligence has paid off—they have succeeded in exercising power in the party far disproportionate to their numbers.

As hard-working and earnest as these fringe folks are, however, they could not drive the debate on these issues without the concurrence of lots of political panderers. A sizable number of pollsters, consultants, and other political pros have concluded that these proposed intrusions into our freedoms are useful wedge issues, issues that can be used to divide people and reinforce intergroup tensions. This theory holds that white males are angry at the perceived threat to their historic social dominance. With the economy globalizing, technology outstripping our ability to comprehend it, our children behaving in ways we no longer understand, the "evil empire" (the Soviet Union) gone—others among us just need new enemies. All of us need folks to blame for what ails us, and even more important, we need nice simple solutions—quick fixes that promise to restore our lost equilibrium.

The pundits see the strategic value of positions that promise us security over liberty. If such positions represent a departure from the historic principles of the Republican party—well, winning comes first.

I am reminded of Joan Rivers's line, "Can we talk?" We Republicans need to talk to each other about the role we really want our government to play in our lives. We need to define the real issues and refuse to respond to the phony ones. We need to acknowledge that many problems are complicated, and that people of good will may differ about their solution. We need to stop demonizing people with whom we disagree. A little intellectual honesty and a decent respect for the Constitution and Bill of Rights would go a long way toward eliminating the political cynicism that threatens to overwhelm public debate.

Newt Gingrich and his troops want to return "voluntary" prayer to the public schools? Truly voluntary prayer is absolutely legal now. What is not legal is government-sponsored prayer, government endorsement of particular religious beliefs. Is it really "satanic" to insist on the freedom of conscience promised by the First Amendment? Is my resistance to government dictating my beliefs and my spirituality hostility to religion? Or is it respect for my own moral autonomy and for the right of others to hold religious convictions at odds with my own?

And what about the wide differences among religious groups when it comes to abortion? Poll after poll confirms that while Americans are conflicted about abortion itself, large majorities believe that government has no business telling individual women what to do. Have the proponents of government control over the most intimate decisions we make ever stopped to consider the implication of granting such power to those we elect? What if a future administration decides that population pressures must be controlled by requiring abortions? The government that decides today I may not abort can decide tomorrow that I must.

For that matter, why is government interference illegitimate in my boardroom, but perfectly okay in my bedroom? Whose business is it whether a soldier is straight or gay? If the soldier misbehaves—sexually harasses someone, for example—he or she should certainly be disciplined, but that should occur irrespective of whether the harassment is of the same or opposite sex. Why are we spending our tax dollars to expel perfectly good officers whose only offense is a sexual identity that differs from our own?

And what do we make of the politicians who insist that they believe in freedom of expression, but who want government to outlaw expression they find offensive? A large number of our elected representatives signed on to the proposed flag-burning amendment. Now, I'll admit I find flag burning very offensive. But I am also offended by bigotry. Some feminists are offended by pornography. Muslims are offended by Salman Rushdie's *Satanic Verses.* Shall we carve out exceptions to the First Amendment whenever enough people find particular ideas or images distasteful? Shall we vote on which books and movies are acceptable and have government suppress the rest?

In our system, we the people get to decide what prayers we say, what books we read, what ideas we endorse. We get to decide when and whether to have children, and whom we love. The government does not get to take a poll or hold an election to make those decisions for us.

My party used to understand that. We used to believe that "the government that governs least, governs best" is a principle to be applied even when *we* are the government. But we seem to have lost our philosophical moorings over the past few years.

The deep divisions caused by the Republican party's

move to the right have not happened overnight, but they were really confirmed—and prominently displayed —in 1992. That year's presidential election hadn't even been held when the "spin doctors" on both sides of the schism began pre-emptive strikes. Those who had controlled the convention and thus much of the public rhetoric attributed George Bush's defeat to an insufficiently fervent embrace of their agenda. (Had he been a "true" conservative, he would have prevailed, according to that view.) Others of us blamed defeat in large measure on his near-total capitulation to those same elements. No one engaged in the debate, however, denied that 1992 was a year when the always uneasy alliance between the Religious Right and the rest of the Republican party began to fall apart. The 1996 elections bore testimony to the damage. From the head of the ticket to state and local races, the tensions between traditional Republicans and the cultural conservatives complicated decision-making and offended interest groups on both sides. Pat Buchanan's primary campaign antagonized those he scorned as "Country Club Republicans"; it also illuminated the philosophical divide between traditional Republicans and the populist right. If his positions were diametrically opposed to historical Republicanism, Buchanan was a least internally consistent; he advocated government intrusion in *both* personal and economic behaviors. He favored measures that would criminalize abortion and outlaw free trade.

While Buchanan's appeal was limited, his supporters were numerous enough (30 percent in some primaries) that they had to be wooed. If they stayed home, many Republican candidates would lose. So Bob Dole's presidential campaign publicly returned a contribution from the gay Log Cabin Republicans, in an obvious attempt to placate Buchanan sympathizers, only to have Dole apologize just as publicly a few weeks later when mainstream Republican criticism could no longer be ignored. Prochoice and antichoice Republicans threatened to desert the ticket if their demands were not met. Both camps watched contested primaries for evidence of the influence of the other. Except in districts dominated by one wing of the party, candidates found it nearly impossible to bridge the gap, and to get out the usual Republican vote.

The current battle within the party is variously described as pitting "purists" against "pragmatists," or "conservatives" against "moderates." I would characterize it as a struggle between libertarian and statist Republicanism. I would further submit that (1) statism, the concentration of power in the government, is philosophically inconsistent with the basic Republican commitment to limited government, and (2) it was the party's avowed commitment to limiting the power of the state that produced successes for the GOP in 1994, as it has before.

Framing the debate in this way assumes, as I do, that ideology is important, and that the American public deserves to choose between alternatives that differ in meaningful (but not necessarily radical) ways. The conflict within the party is not a contest between those who believe we should "stand for something" and those who would blur ideological distinctions. Rather, it grows out of a profound and probably irreconcilable dispute over just what it is that conservatives should "stand for." It is a contest between the libertarian philosophy of Barry Goldwater and the theocratic philosophy of Pat Robertson.

Available data strongly suggests that the strength of the Republican party has derived in large measure from our position that when individuals are allowed to make their own decisions—economic, intellectual, or moral—we will produce a robust and vital polity. Republicans have thus "stood for" the proposition that individuals be given the maximum amount of personal liberty consistent with the maintenance of social order.

The abiding belief of Republicans in limited government should not be confused with a predilection to anarchy. As a party, we have always accepted that there is an appropriate role for government. In a free society, the State is the mechanism through which individuals achieve social goals for which there exist a broad public consensus. There may even be certain jobs that government can do more effectively than can private enterprise—although it has been an article of faith that such situations are rare, and as Republicans we have insisted that the case had better be made convincingly. Republicans are seldom if ever among those insisting that "government knows best." In close cases, we have traditionally favored individual freedom over governmental power even when that power is being exercised with the best of intentions and the individual freedom poses social risks.

The current struggle is between the legitimate heirs of that philosophy and those who would apply it only in an economic context—those who are prepared, even eager, to use government to impose their own religious/cultural/moral beliefs on others. These "cultural conservatives" are unwilling to engage in intellectual battle in the marketplace of ideas, where they have evidently concluded they cannot win. (This, of course, is not attributed to any flaw in their positions, which are generally described as divinely inspired. Usually, the lack of popular acceptance is attributed to an overwhelmingly biased and presumably monolithic media, to moral corruption, public schools, and of course, the

ACLU.) In their zeal to enact their religious preferences into law, they ignore a fundamental premise Republicans have historically understood: that while popular passion is not a sufficient basis for legislation, laws enacted without broad consensus undermine the very social authority that makes the rule of law possible.

The same people who argue persuasively against government encroachment in private business decisions, who point to the deadening effect of runaway bureaucracy, who apparently understand that there can be no political freedom without economic freedom—these same people are perfectly willing to grant to *government* the authority to regulate our most personal behaviors and beliefs. (Of course, they are willing to give government such power only if it is used to advance *their* agendas.) Suddenly, the party is captive to a movement that is prepared to trade away our most fundamental liberties in exchange for legislation promoting its own special vision of righteousness. Every totalitarian regime has justified its power by claiming some overwhelming moral imperative. The genius of American constitutional government has been an insistence on the integrity and inviolability of the individual conscience. The Republican party has been most principled and most successful when it has emphasized that fundamental ethic of individual moral responsibility.

So much for ideology. What will happen to a Republican party where the Pat Robertsons and Pat Buchanans are in control? What message will the GOP then send to prospective voters?

- It will be philosophically and intellectually inconsistent and thus unpersuasive. By taking a position that government does not belong in the boardroom but does belong in the bedroom, we open ourselves to the charge that we are not proponents of freedom at all—merely apologists for our own special interests.

- Most Americans understand—viscerally, if not conceptually—that government is a dangerous tool for social engineering, or for imposing cultural conformity. That understanding—that healthy distrust—has been a source of great strength for the GOP. By embracing the agenda of the radical right, we abandon it.

- Despite the tensions among groups in our society, most Americans are uncomfortable with public displays of bigotry, and no matter how the apologists try to dress it up, bigotry is what millions of Americans saw at the 1992 Republican convention in Houston, and what they have seen from a number of the freshmen swept into Congress in 1994. One need not be anti-Christian to reject attempts to turn America into a "Christian nation" where Jews, Hindus, Muslims, and others are second-class citizens. One need not be "antifamily" to believe that bigotry against gays and lesbians is wrong or to find the personal attacks on the Clintons distasteful. People with positive ideas to sell do not need to resort to personal nastiness. By engaging in mean-spirited rhetoric, by demonizing those with whom we disagree, we signal the poverty of our message.

So long as the Republican party is controlled by those whose goal is division and whose method is the moral litmus test—by those who approach all issues with an "us" versus "them" mentality—we will repel rather than attract. In 1992, while Republicans were deciding who was fit to enter our ever-shrinking tent, Bill Clinton won election by talking about unifying America, bringing people together, and repairing, rather than exacerbating, our differences. Ronald Reagan always understood the power of images of inclusiveness and reconciliation. In fact, his was one of the few speeches in Houston that was free of smarmy self-righteousness.

I believe that a commitment to limited government and civil liberties is most likely to produce a just and prosperous society. That belief is what attracted me to the ACLU, and it is what attracted me (and many others) to the Republican party. If the party abandons its commitment to that philosophy, it abandons and disenfranchises those of us who have worked long and hard to advance both the party and those fundamental principles.

16

The American Idea: Summing Up

★★

America is more an *idea* than a place.

Ours was the first nation not to be based upon geography, ethnicity, or conquest, but upon a theory of social organization. That theory—that idea—was incorporated in our constituent documents: the Declaration of Independence, the Constitution, and the Bill of Rights. It has provided the basis for Republican philosophy and for the mission of the ACLU.

One might argue that America is therefore uniquely situated to thrive in a world where trade and technology are making geography increasingly irrelevant; where travel, immigration, and economic trends are forcing diversification of even the most insular societies; and where armed conquest is increasingly unthinkable.

The American idea reflected certain assumptions and incorporated certain values. While some of these assumptions are currently being called into question, the underlying values were—and are—sound and ought to be more explicitly recognized, discussed, and understood. Those values provide the common ground for our citizenship; they define our "public morality." Understanding them is fundamental to our ability to understand ourselves and to construct a civic and civil society.

This thesis does not assume that the founders spoke with one voice, or embraced a single worldview. All of our governing documents were the result of passionate argument and eventual compromise. Neither were the founders infallible. As remarkable as their achievement was, as enduring as the bulk of their work has proven to be, the system they established was not perfect, nor was it sufficient for all time.

Constitutional scholars and media pundits frequently refer to the "original intent" of the founders. There are those who believe that the role of the courts is to ascertain that original intent and apply it— nothing more. Such a view of the judicial function arguably misreads history; in any event, it is impossible. Whose "original intent" are we to apply? John Marshall's? Thomas Jefferson's? James Madison's? How are we to determine what that intent really was?

More to the point, constitutions are by their nature statements of basic principles to be applied to fact situations which may or may not be foreseeable at the time the principles are enunciated. Our inquiry, properly understood, must be to discern the principle, or value, involved and apply it to a rapidly changing world. The question is not what did James Madison say about controlling pornography in cyberspace? It is a safe assumption that James Madison never considered the issue. Courts today must look at the *value* that the First Amendment places upon the protection of expressive freedoms against government interference and decide how those principles should apply to this new technology.

The great debates between the Federalists and Antifederalists were about the proper role of government and the nature of the so-called inalienable rights that each citizen should enjoy. The debates continue today. While we have enlarged our notion of citizenship since the constitutional convention (we now include women, former slaves, and non-landowners) the framework remains the same. The overarching issue is the nature of the balance between state power and individual autonomy. It is the issue that has preoccupied traditional Republicans and civil libertarians alike. The issue, in our system, is who decides? Who decides what book you read, what prayer you say, whom you marry, how you use your property? Who decides when the state may deprive you of your liberty? How do we balance government's right to exercise authority and enforce order against the individual's right to be secure in his person and free in his conscience? The founders answered that question by carving out, in the Bill of Rights, actions government was forbidden to take. The Bill of Rights *reserved* certain fundamental rights to the citizens and in some instances to the states. Individual liberty was an overriding value, to be circumscribed only when absolutely necessary.

Today, the individual rights secured to citizens by the Bill of Rights are under attack from both the Right and Left. It is instructive to examine the basis of that attack. Generally, the argument is made that the United States has gone "too far" toward individualism and individual liberties. This theory holds that too much autonomy on the part of citizens erodes our sense of community and damages the "rights" of the majority. In this view, the good of the whole must take precedence over the rights of individual members of society. It is a view that the ACLU and libertarian Republicans have always rejected.

The difficulty with this argument is that a community in the truest sense cannot exist unless it is based upon respect for the rights of each of its individual members. While one can certainly debate the merits of certain court decisions or the emphases the courts have placed on particular rights, the notion of equality of all citizens before the law is an essential condition of a just society. If citizens have equal rights and if those rights must be respected both by government and by other citizens, they must be defined, agreed upon, and publicly acknowledged.

What are the "rights" of the majority as distinct from the rights of individual citizens? How do we determine them? When we ask the question, we immediately see that there are two very different answers possible. In a totally majoritarian system, the rights of the majority at any given time are what the majority decides they are. In such a system, the only issue will be one of accuracy and definition: What shall constitute a majority for purposes of legitimizing the use of state power? How can we be certain the votes accurately reflect citizen sentiment? Who shall have the right to vote? In a truly majoritarian system, the voters would have the right to decide what books could be printed and sold, which religious practices would be tolerated, how much authority police could exercise, and so forth. The only limits to government's power over individuals would be those sanctioned from time to time by the voters, and those limits could be changed at any time by a subsequent vote. A truly majoritarian system would certainly reflect "community values" at any given time. It would also—necessarily—impose those values on those who do not share them. Holders of minority opinions, dissenters from the prevailing wisdom, would have no recognized or enforceable right to be different.

Such a system is precisely what the founders feared: this is what they meant by "the tyranny of the majority."

The second answer to the question of majority rights is the one chosen by the founders of our republic. In the system they established, the rights of the majority are derivative of our individual liberties: the right to participate equally with one's peers to make decisions which are properly assigned to majority vote; the right to be protected from those who would threaten our physical safety or otherwise deprive us of social benefits to which we are entitled; the right to have our agreements with each other enforced and our disagreements mediated—all without favoritism or bias. And of course, there is the right which Justice Louis Brandeis once called the greatest right conferred by a civilized society—the right to be left alone.

History provides us plenty of examples of what happens when the "good of the many" is piously invoked to outweigh the rights of individuals. A paraphrase from George Orwell's brilliant satire *Animal Farm* sums it up best: Everyone is equal but some are more equal than others.[1] Today we see groups on the political right who "know best" what books we should read, what prayers we should say, whom we should love. We see groups on the political left endorsing "hate speech" legislation and censorship of materials which they believe are (or ought to be) offensive to women. Both want to use the power of the state to impose "goodness" on the rest of us. The problem is, they want to be the ones who define goodness. Absolutely basic to our form of government is an assumption that they may not do so—that so long as they do not harm others, individuals have the right to make their own decisions, *even when most people believe those decisions to be wrong.* Freedom necessarily includes the right to be wrong.

When people fail to understand that the central issue is one of power, they frequently confuse support for constitutional rights with support for unpopular uses of those rights. If the issue is who decides what book you read, support for your right to make that decision free of governmental interference is not mistaken for endorsement of your choice of reading material. If the issue is framed less carefully—or less honestly—the argument focuses upon the wisdom or propriety of your choice. It is important to make the distinction: The issue is your right to make choices for yourself, free of government coercion. A lawyer who represents a child molester is not "endorsing" child molestation. He or she is upholding the right of each citizen to the due process of law. An insistence on a woman's right to choose abortion is not the equivalent of a "proabortion" position—many women who oppose abortion do not believe that government has the right to make that decision for individual women. An insistence on freedom for the press certainly does not translate into approval of all that the press may choose to print. Eighteenth-century French author Voltaire summed it up nicely in his famous statement: "I disagree with what you say but I will defend to the death your right to say it." The central issue for civil libertarians and traditional Republicans is the power of the state, or the majority, to compel our behavior or infringe our liberties.

Of course, individual rights carry with them civic responsibilities. One reason citizenship was originally conferred only upon landowners was the founders' belief that citizenship required a proper understanding of one's responsibilities, and the elitist notion that only "substantial" folks were prepared to assume those burdens of citizenship.

While the American legal system and the American media frame most issues in terms of the rights involved, the lack of emphasis on responsibilities should not obscure their importance. The entire system depends upon the willingness of citizens to exercise responsibility: to display the public morality without which government and society cannot function. Just as the media focuses on crime, rarely commenting on the incidents of lawful behavior which are far more common, we tend to pay far more attention to social pathologies than we do to the fact that most Americans continue to demonstrate the values and civic virtues necessary to the maintenance of an open and orderly society.

As a society, we expect parents to support and instruct their children; we expect homeowners to be responsible for their property; we expect employers and employees to discharge their respective duties. We expect to hold criminals responsible for their crimes. In a system that accords people rights, we necessarily depend upon those people to act responsibly. It is what we do when people don't meet our expectations that defines our commitment to civil liberties and the American legal system.

Unfortunately, there is no scarcity of opinion favoring a totalitarian response. Parents won't monitor what their kids are watching on TV? Have government ban inappropriate material—after government decides what material that is. Are children not getting proper religious instruction? Make the public schools require them to pray. Too much crime and violence? Have government confiscate all the guns and frisk anyone who looks suspicious. Too much bigotry? Pass a law against hate speech.

What is really attractive about these solutions is that they are easy. As we piously attribute the need for government control to other people's deplorable lack of responsibility, we are the ones who are betraying the responsibilities of citizenship in a free society. Instead of sitting in front of a television set complaining that "there ought to be a law" and "someone should do something," responsible citizens in a free society each need to ask ourselves what *we* are doing. What responsibilities have *we* assumed? When someone said something bigoted in your presence, did you express your disapproval? When something on television offended you, did you write the sponsor? The television station? If you saw a neighbor child neglected, did you call the appropriate agency? Have you joined crime watch in your neighborhood? Have you volunteered to work with youth at your church, synagogue, mosque, or other place of worship? At the neighborhood school?

If free people do not take personal responsibility, pretty soon they are no longer free. There are no shortcuts. Both civil libertarians and libertarian Republicans understand that when we hand over to government the power to impose "correct" behavior, we have effectively surrendered both liberty and moral autonomy. If we are to avoid such surrender, Americans must understand, accept, and act upon the civic values that constitute our "public morality."

What are those values? How can we summarize them?

There is the value of liberty. Americans believe in our inalienable right to hold our own opinions, to think for ourselves, to assemble with our friends, to cast our votes, to pray or not, all free of government coercion.

There is the value of equality before the law. This is not to be confused with the fuzzy notion that we are all somehow interchangeable. It is not to be confused with the belief of some religions that all people are equally worthwhile. This is a more limited proposition—the notion that government must apply the same rules to all its citizens, that groups do not have rights, individuals do. It was a radical notion in 1776. It is fundamental to the way we understand ourselves and our society today.

We value the marketplace of ideas, the supreme importance of our ability to communicate with each other, unfettered by government censorship.

We value government legitimacy and the rule of law. So long as our representatives continue to derive their authority from the consent of those they govern, we recognize our individual obligations to respect and obey the law. If we protest a law we believe to be unjust, we recognize our obligation to accept the consequences of that disobedience.

Finally, we value the civic virtues which are necessary to the realization of the foregoing values: honesty, courage, kindness, civility, mutual respect, and tolerance.

In a country where, increasingly, people read different books and magazines, watch different television shows, attend different churches, and even speak different languages—where the information and beliefs we all share are diminishing and our variety and diversity are growing—these are the core values we can identify, agree upon, and teach our children.

With all its flaws, America is an achievement of the human spirit. That achievement rests on a unique idea: the power of the state must be constrained. This overarching belief in individual liberty and limited government has characterized the history and ideology of both the Republican party and the American Civil Liberties Union. Conventional wisdom to the contrary, libertarian Republicans are the ACLU's staunchest allies in defense of the American Idea.

NOTE

1. George Orwell, *Animal Farm* (New York: Harcourt Brace & Co., 1946).